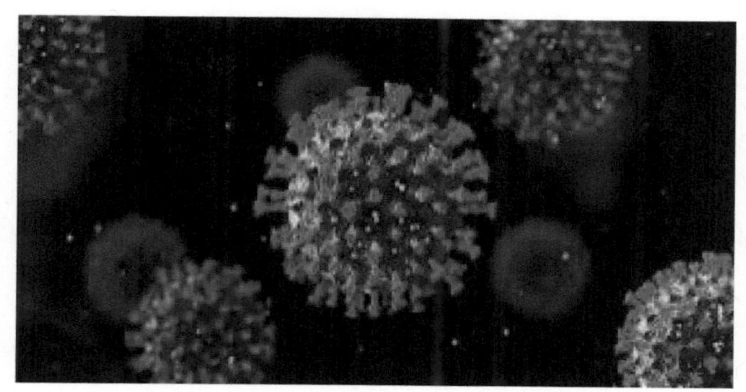

# GENESIS OF COVID-19:

## A MAN MADE VIRUS

DEO DATTA SINGH

# PREFACE

*This work is dedicated to seven million people, who lost their lives in the COVID-19 pandemic of December 2019 period. In this book, I have tried to give complete evidences for or against the hypothesis for the origin of COVID-19, as natural virus or man made. The readers will* ***give their opinion in this regard. I have given both sides of evidences.These are based on scientific as well as logic evidences, although in science logic evidence has no meaning. But in the case,if the original data is destroyed; in such case we have to make our own judgement about the truth finding process using our brain.***

*We acknowledge and sincerely thank of the following journals for the article used in this book:*

*(i)Research article : Open Access*

*Published: 21 January 202PREFACE1*

*Horizontal gene transfer and recombination analysis of SARS-CoV-2 genes helps discover its close relatives and shed light on its origin*

*Vladimir Makarenkov, Bogdan Mazoure, Guillaume Rabusseau & Pierre Legendre BMC Ecology and Evolution volume 21, Article number: 5 (2021) Cite this article ;https://doi.org/10.1186/s12862-*

*I have got my inspiration for this work from LORD JESUS CHRIST, whose virtual inspiration and support has given me for this book. I have worked in SEISMOLOGY for about 34 years and published 35 research papers in international journals of high standard on various research problems of seismology.*

***DEO DATTA SINGH (AUTHOR)***

***CHAPTER I***

***SUMMARY ……7***

***Definition of terms used in COVID-19 11***

***CHAPTER II***

***Terms used in VIROLOGY …24***

***Controlling and prevention of Disease …27***

*The HOST ....31*
*Zoonosis(transmissio from animal to person) ...29*
*Carriers hosts without obvious illness ...27*
*Transmission of disease ...32*
*Controlling and preventing disease ...34*
*Disease and disease transmission ...34*
*CHAPTER III*
*Origin of Virus ...72*
*Status of virus in living world ..75*
*Viruses with large Genomes ...74*
*The concept of Tree of life (TOL)..78*
*CHAPTER IV*
*Virul Culture ..81*
*Procedure of virus cultivation in cell lines ...85*
*CHAPTER V*
*COVID-19 ...88*
*Origin of COVID-19 ...94*
*CHAPTER VI*
*Role of COVID-19 in Heart attack ...113*
*ACE2 Receptor ....117*
*Mechanisms of cardiac damage in COVID-19 ...118*
*Receptor Blockers(ARB) convalescent plasma ..122*
*Heart failure ...123*
*Arrhythmias and sudden cardiac arrest ..126*
*Thromboembolism and coagulation abnormalities ...131*
*Accute cornary syndrome ...134*
*Myocardial injury ..135*
*Heat*
*failure ...137*
*Electcardiogram ..145*
*Cardiovascular magnetic resonance ...149*
*CHAPTER VII*

*Gene edition ..160*
*FURIN .. 162*
*CRISPR-Cas9 …164*
*Application of the crispr system ..167*
*Gene silencing and editing with CRISPR ..169*
*CHAPTER VIII*
*GENETIC ENGINEERING …185*
*Benefits of genetic engineering …189*
*Spike proteins ..193*
*Gene therapy …197*
*CHAPTER IX*
*Mysterious ORIGIN of COVID -19 .219*
*Bat viruses displaced …221*
*CHAPTER X*
*REFERENCESAB .. 230*
*SUMMARY …232*
*Corona-19 Virus brief description ..238*
*REFERENCE…..243*

## *GENESIS OF COVID-19:A MAN MADE VIRUS*

## *SUMMARY*

***Majority of scientists established the result that COVID-19 from the Genome sequence analysis is a natural virus and very few scientists found from experimental result of COVID-19 virus as a laboratory derived from the culture of corona virus, which appeared in 2002-2003 in 28 different countries and killed about 800 persons. But the present COVID-19 virus which appeared in December 2019 in China had great***

*transmissibility and infectivity rate compared to 2002-2003 corona virus. This can not be created from the culture of virus, as it can give mutation of virus only and infectivity and transmissibility rate can not achieved in a tremendous way. For this we propose the theory of origin of COVID-19 virus. In* **this theory,** the *Genome Editing tool (CRISPR-Cas9) has been used to the novel CORONAVIRUS (nCoV) ,which appeared in 2002-2003 in GUANDONG Province of CHINA with the inclusion of some of the constrains of INFLUENZA, MALARIA, EBOLA and AIDS viruses by the scientists of the Microbiology Research institute using the Biological Scissor. This type of Genome editing and inclusion of FOUR Viruses ( some of the constrains of INFLUENZA, MALARIA,EBOLA and AIDS, respectively) in the novel CORONOVIRUS is possible in Microbiological Laboratory only, as the scientists are doing research work in CONONOVIRUS since 2000 beginning itself and they are expert in this field and have the technical and scientific know how sufficiently in this type of research problem.* **COVID-19 contains an uncommon genetic sequence that has been used by genetic engineers in the past to insert genes into corona virus( 26 to 32 kilobases) without leaving a trace, and it falls at the exact point that would allow experimenters to swap out different genetic parts to change the infection and transmissibility . That same sequence can occur naturally in a corona virus. The Genome Editing tool (CRISPR-Cas9) has been used to the novel CORONAVIRUS (nCoV) ,which appeared in 2002-2003 in GUANDONG Province of CHINA with the**

**inclusion of some of the constrains of INFLUENZA,MALARIA, EBOLA and AIDS viruses to increase the infectivity and transmissiblity in a tremendous manner to spread throughout the world .**

**In addition to this, there are other several unique features that point out the fact that SARS-CoV-2 corona virus was a MAN MADE VIRUS, rather than emerging through natural spillover from animals. They are as follows:**

**(i) CORONA-19 Viruses are considered to be non- living due to the characteristics like (a)They lack metabolic activity outside the living cells.(b)They lack cellular organism. Once they infect a cell they take over the machinery of the host cell to replicate themselves. (c)They lack ribosomes and cellular enzymes necessary for nucleic acid and protein synthesis. (d) They don't show cell division, growth, development ,nutrition etc.(e) They can be crystallized .(f) They don't contain both RNA and DNA together.**

**(ii)The presence of the spike glycoprotein and a novel lineage B betacoronavirus (βCoV), has caused a global pandemic of coronavirus disease (COVID-19).**

**(iii) It has been speculated that RRAR, a unique furin-like cleavage site (FCS) in the spike protein (S), and it is absent in other lineage B βCoVs, such as SARS-CoV, is responsible for its high infectivity and transmissibility.**

**(iv) The report given by Dr. Li-Meng Yan of HongKong Public Health Department states that SARS-CoV-2 is "suspiciously" similar to two strains of bat coronaviruses,**

**called ZC45 and ZXC21, that were discovered by scientists at military labs in China. The authors claim these strains could have been used as a template to clone a deadlier virus. But other scientists do not support this idea.**

**(v) phylogenetic analysis of SARS-CoV-2 identified an insertion of RRAR (FCS) at the S1/S2 site of SARS-CoV-2-S, which is absent in SARS-CoV and other SARS-related coronaviruses (SARSr-CoVs), family. It is the seventh known coronavirus to infect humans; four of these coronaviruses (229E, NL63, particularly RaTG13, which has 96% identity of its genomic sequence to that of SARS-CoV-2 The COVID-19 is acute respiratory syndrome coronavirus 2 (SARS-CoV-2), which belongs to the β coronavirus OC43, and HKU1) only cause slight symptoms of the common cold. Conversely, the other three, SARS-CoV, MERS-CoV, and SARS-CoV-2, are able to cause severe symptoms and even death, with fatality rates of 10%, 37%, and 5%, respectively. The inclusion of strains of EBOLA, INFLUENZA, MALARIA, AIDS viruses in the CORONAVIRUS (nCoV) has increased its transmissibility and infectivity in a tremendous way to spread COVID -19 throughout the world and killing more than 8 million people ( official data), but the actual data is about 20 million death.**

**(vi) The SARS-CoV-2 has "restriction-enzyme sites," or genetic sequences that can be cut and manipulated by enzymes. These genomic features are sometimes used in cloning, and the report claims their presence is indicative of an engineered virus. But scientists point out these sites**

**naturally occur in all types of genomes, from bacteria to humans.**

# Definition of terms used in COVID-19:

**The pathogen is an organism that causes the infection. Different pathogens cause different infections; e.g. Cholera is caused by the bacterium *Vibrio cholerae*, , and Leishmaniasis is caused by different species (spp.) of the protozoa**
***Leishmania*.**
**Different categories of pathogens can infect human. The pathogens causing the diseases covered include viruses, bacteria, rickettsiae, fungi, proto-zoa, and helminths (worms). All pathogens go through a lifecycle, which takes the organism from reproducing adult to reproducing adult. This cycle includes phases of growth, consolidation, change of structure, multiplication/reproduction, spread, and infection of a new host. The combination of these phases is called the development of the pathogen.**

**Mutation is defined as a single change in a virus's genome (genetic code). It happens frequently, but only sometimes changes the characteristics of the**

**Recombinant is defined as process in which the infected a person at the same time) combine during the viral replication process to form a new variant that is different from both parent lineages.**

**Lineage is a group of closely related viruses with a common ancestor. SARS-CoV-2 has many lineages; all cause COVID-19.**

**Variant is a viral genome (genetic code) that may contain one or more mutations. In some cases, a group of variants with similar genetic changes, such as a lineage or group of lineages, may be designated by public health organizations as a Variant Being Monitored (VBM), Variant of Concern (VOC) or a Variant of Interest (VOI) due to shared attributes and characteristics that may require public health action.**

## Different characteristics associated with COVID-19:

**(i) Genetic lineages of SARS-CoV-2 have been emerging and circulating around the world since the beginning of the COVID-19 pandemic.**

**(ii) SARS-CoV-2 genetic lineages in the United States are routinely monitored through epidemiological**

**investigations, virus genetic sequence-based surveillance, and laboratory studies.**

**(iii) On November 30, 2021, the U.S. government SARS-CoV-2 Inter agency Group (SIG) classified Omicron as a Variant of Concern (VOC). This classification was based on the following criteria:**

**(i) Detection of cases attributed to Omicron in multiple countries, including among those**

**(ii) without travel history.**

**(iii) Transmission and replacement of the Delta variant in South Africa.**

**(iv) The number and locations of substitutions in the spike protein.**

**(iv) Available data for other variants with fewer substitutions in the spike protein that indicate a reduction in neutralization by sera from vaccinated or convalescent individuals.**

**(v) Available data for other variants with fewer substitutions in the spike protein that indicate reduced susceptibility to certain monoclonal antibody treatments.**

**(vi) On April 14, 2022 the U.S government SARS-CoV-2 Inter-agency Group (SIG) downgraded Delta from a Variant of Concern to a Variant Being Monitored. This new classification was based on the following:**

(i) Significant and sustained reduction in its national and regional proportions over time.

(ii) Evidence suggesting that Delta does not currently pose a significant risk to public health in the United States.

(iii) The SIG Variant classification scheme defines four classes of SARS-CoV-2 variants:

There are different classifications of variant done by international organization(WHO). They are as follows:

(i) Alpha (B.1.1.7 and Q lineages)

(ii) Beta (B.1.351 and descendent lineages)

(iii) Gamma (P.1 and descendent lineages)

(iv) Delta (B.1.617.2 and AY lineages)

(v) Epsilon (B.1.427 and B.1.429)

(vi) Eta (B.1.525)

(vii) Iota (B.1.526)

(viii) Kappa (B.1.617.1)

(ix) 1.617.3

(x) Mu (B.1.621, B.1.621.1)

(xi) Zeta (P.2)

Variant of Concern (VOC) are

Omicron (B.1.1.529, BA.1, BA.1.1, BA.2, BA.3, BA.4 and BA.5 lineages)

## Method of classification of variant:

The U.S. Department of Health and Human Services (HHS) established a SARS-CoV-2 Inter-agency Group (SIG) to enhance coordination among CDC, National Institutes of Health (NIH), Food and Drug Administration (FDA), Biomedical Advanced Research and Development Authority (BARDA), and Department of Defense (DoD). This inter-agency group is focused on the rapid characterization of emerging variants and actively monitors their potential impact on critical SARS-CoV-2 countermeasures, including vaccines, therapeutics, and diagnostics.

The SIG meets regularly to evaluate the risk posed by SARS-CoV-2 variants circulating in the United States and to make recommendations about the classification of variants. This evaluation is undertaken by a group of subject matter experts who assess available data, including variant proportions at the national and regional levels and the potential or known impact of the constellation of mutations on the effectiveness of medical countermeasures, severity of disease, and ability to spread from person to person. Given the continuous evolution of SARS-CoV-2 and our understanding of the impact of variants on public health, variants may be reclassified based on their attributes and prevalence in the United States.

These variants continue to be closely monitored to identify changes in their proportions and new data are continually being analyzed. If the data indicate that a VBM warrants more concern, the classification will be changed based on the SIG assessment of the attributes of the variant and the risk to public health in the United States.

According to WHO, there are various variants identified. They are as follows (WHO DATA):

| | B.1.1.7 and Q lineages | |
|---|---|---|
| Beta | | |
| | | |
| Delta | | |
| | | |
| | B.1.351 and descendent lineages | |
| | P.1and descendent lineages | |
| | B.1.617.2 and AY lineages | |
| | B.1.427<br>B.1.429 | |
| Eta | B.1.525 | |
| Iota | B.1.526 | |
| Kappa | B.1.617.1 | |
| N/A | B.1.617.3 | |
| Zeta | P.2 | |
| Mu | B.1.621, B.1.621.1 | |

| | | |
|---|---|---|

*Variant of Interest (VOI)*

***A variant with specific genetic markers that have been associated with changes to receptor binding, reduced neutralization by antibodies generated against previous infection or vaccination, reduced efficacy of treatments, potential diagnostic impact, or predicted increase in admissibility or disease severity.***

***Possible attributes of a Variant of Interest are classified as follows:***

**(i) Specific genetic markers that are predicted to affect transmission, diagnostics, therapeutics, or immune escape.**

**(ii) Evidence that it is the cause of an increased proportion of cases or unique outbreak clusters.**

**(iii) Limited prevalence or expansion in the US or in other countries.**

**A Variant of Interest might require one or more appropriate public health**

**actions, including enhanced sequence surveillance, enhanced laboratory characterization, or epidemiological investigations to assess how easily the virus spreads to others, the severity of disease, the efficacy of therapeutics and whether currently approved or authorized vaccines offer protection.**

**Currently, no SARS-CoV-2 variants are designated as VOI.**

Variant of Concern (VOC)

**A variant for which there is evidence of an increase in transmissibility, more severe disease (for example, increased hospitalizations or deaths), significant reduction in neutralization by antibodies generated during previous infection or vaccination, reduced effectiveness of treatments or vaccines, or diagnostic**

**detection failures.**

In addition to the possible attributes of a variant of interest are as follows:

**(i) Evidence of impact on diagnostics, treatments, or vaccines**
**(ii) Widespread interference with diagnostic test targets**
**(iii) Evidence of substantially decreased susceptibility to one or more class of therapies**
**(iv) Evidence of significantly decreased neutralization by antibodies generated during previous infection or vaccination**
**(v) Evidence of reduced vaccine-induced protection from severe disease**
**(vi) Evidence of increased transmissibility**
**(vii) Evidence of increased disease severity**

**Variants of concern might require one or more appropriate public health actions, such as notification to WHO under the International Health Regulations, reporting to CDC, local or regional efforts to control spread, increased testing, or research to determine the effectiveness of vaccines and treatments against the variant. Based on the characteristics of the variant, additional considerations may include the development of new diagnostics or the modification of vaccines or treatments.**

**Current variants of concern in the United States that are being closely monitored and characterized are listed below. This table will be updated when a new variant of concern is identified.**

**Pango Lineage: B.1.1.529, BA.1, BA.1.1, BA.2, BA.3, BA.4 and BA.5 lineages (Pango lineage)a**

**Spike Protein Substitutions: A67V, del69-70, T95I, del142-144, Y145D, del211, L212I, ins214EPE, G339D, S371L, S373P, S375F, K417N, N440K, G446S, S477N, T478K, E484A, Q493R, G496S, Q498R, N501Y, Y505H, T547K, D614G, H655Y, N679K, P681H, N764K, D796Y, N856K, Q954H, N969K, L981F**

**Nextstrain clade (Nextstrain)b: 21K**

**First Identified: South Africa**

**Attributes:**

- **Potential increased transmissibility**
- **Potential reduction in neutralization by some EUA monoclonal antibody treatments**
- **Potential reduction in neutralization by post-vaccination sera**

Variant of High Consequence (VOHC)

**A VOHC has clear evidence that prevention measures**

**or medical countermeasures (MCMs) have significantly reduced effectiveness relative to previously circulating**

**variants.**

**Possible attributes of a variant of high consequence:**

In addition to the possible attributes of a variant of concern

- **Impact on MCMs**

**Demonstrated failure of diagnostic test targets**

**Evidence to suggest a significant reduction in vaccine effectiveness, a disproportionately high number of infections in vaccinated persons, or very low vaccine-induced protection against severe disease**

- **Significantly reduced susceptibility to multiple EUA or approved therapeutics**
- **More severe clinical disease and increased hospitalizations**

**A variant of high consequence would require notification to WHO under the International Health Regulations, reporting to CDC, an announcement of strategies to prevent or contain transmission, and recommendations to update treatments and vaccines.**

- Emerging SARS-CoV-2 Variants

---

**Severe acute respiratory syndrome coronavirus 2 (SARS-CoV-2) is causing a pandemic of coronavirus disease since December 2019 (COVID-19). The worldwide transmission of COVID-19 from human to human is spreading like wildfire, affecting almost every country in the world. In the past 100 years, the globe did not face a microbial pandemic similar in scale to COVID-19.**

***We are very much grateful and sincerely thank and very obliged to the*** 

## TERMS USED IN VIROLOGY

### The pathogen:

**The pathogen is the organism that causes the infection. Different pathogens cause different infections. Cholera is caused by the bacterium *Vibrio cholerae*, and Leishmaniasis is caused by different species (spp.) of the protozoa *Leishmania*.**

**Different infections also have specific transmission cycles. To be able to react appropriately to health problems in a population, the specific infection causing the problems must be known. Identification of the infection will usually be done by medical personnel.**

**Different categories of pathogens can infect humans. The pathogens causing the diseases covered in this manual include viruses, bacteria, rickettsiae, fungi, proto-zoa, and helminths (worms). All pathogens go through a lifecycle, which takes the organism from reproducing adult to reproducing adult. This cycle includes phases of growth, consolidation, change of structure, multiplication/reproduction, spread, and infection of a new host. The combination of these phases is called the development of the pathogen.**

**Two terms are commonly used to describe pathogens leaving the host through faeces or urine (i) latency and (ii) persistence.**

**After excretion, a latent pathogen must develop in the environment or intermediate host before a susceptible person or animal can be infected. During the latent period the pathogen is not infectious. A non-latent pathogen does**

**not need to go through a development, and can cause infection directly after being excreted.**

**Persist ency of pathogen is defined as how long a pathogen can survive in the environment. A persistent pathogen remains viable for a long period outside the host (may be few months), while a non-persistent pathogen remains viable for only a limited period such as days, or weeks.**

**Virologists define the active immunity as the resistance the person or animal develops against the pathogen after overcoming infection or through immunization (vaccination). Depending on the pathogen, the effectiveness of active immunity often decreases over time.**

***It is seen that not all infections will cause disease. But in fact, a pathogen may cause illness in one person, it may be killed or cause asymptomatic infection in another.***

## *CONTROLLING AND PREVENTING DISEASE*

**Usually immunity only develops against the specific pathogen that caused the infection. If there are different types (stereotype or strains) of the same pathogen (e.g. in dengue fever and scrub typhus), immunity will often only develop against the particular type which caused the infection. The person or animal can still develop the illness when infected with another stereotype or strain of the pathogen.**

There are different categories of pathogenic organisms with some of their characteristics, including latency, persistence, and immunity. The information is general, and exceptions can occur.

## The host

The host is the person or animal infected by the pathogen. The importance of the host in the transmission cycle is its roles as both reservoir and source of patio-gens.

There are two types of host: definitive and intermediate host. The definitive host is the person or animal infected with the adult, or sexual, form of the pathogen. In the infections covered here, people are usually the definitive host. To keep things simple the definitive host is called just 'the host'.

The intermediate host is an animal or person infected by a larval, or asexual, form of the pathogen. Cholecystitis and hydration disease are the only infections covered here for which people are the intermediate host. Where intermediate host is meant, this term is used. Of the infections covered here, only millionths have both definitive and intermediate hosts. All other pathogens only have definitive hosts, although vectors function technically as intermediate hosts for protozoa.

### *Zoonosis (transmission from animal to person)*

Some pathogens are specific to humans, others to animals. Many pathogens are less specific and can infect both people and animals. Infections that can naturally be transmitted from animal to person are called zoonoses . Zoo noses are very common; over half of the infections covered in this manual are zoo noses. Many of these infections normally occur in an animal cycle, with people being infected by chance.

The problem with zoo noses is that a continuous reservoir of pathogens exists outside humans. Even if all human infections were cured and transmission to people stopped, the presence of an animal reservoir would remain a continuous risk to people.
Prevention of zoonoses often includes control of animal hosts. This is possible by reducing the number of hosts (e.g. controlling rats), immunizing domestic animals, or avoiding unnecessary contact with host animals.

*Carriers: hosts without obvious illness*

A person or animal who develops an illness is an obvious example of a host. It is very common, however,for infections to occur without the disease developing. The person or animal infected can potentially spread the pathogen, but does not show clear symptoms [8]. The symptoms may be mild, or may be completely absent.These hosts are called carriers, or asymptomatic carriers. We show some infections that are frequently mild or asymptomatic. The host can be infectious for a short period in transient carriers, or over a prolonged period in a chronic carrier. Incubating carriers have been infected and can spread the pathogen, but do not yet show the symptoms of the illness. Convalescent carriers continue to spread the pathogen even though they have recovered from illness.

In many infections carriers play an important role in transmitting the pathogen. It is usually not possible to identify asymptomatic carriers , and unless the family and other close contacts of the sick person or even the whole population can be treated, carriers will remain a threat to the health of those surrounding them.

DISEASE AND DISEASE TRANSMISSION

*Other reservoirs of pathogens*

~~Besides hosts, there are several other pathogen~~ reservoirs that can play a role in the transmission of disease. Some

**pathogens are very resistant, and can survive in the environment for considerable time. Though this will normally be an except-tion, roundworm eggs can remain viable in soil for years [3].**

**Intermediate hosts may be important reservoirs of pathogens, and several millionths can even multiply in the intermediate host.**

**Vectors are usually infectious for life, and several pathogens can be transmitted to the offspring of the vector over several generations . A soft tick, for example, can survive for more than five years and can pass to its offspring the pathogen which causes tick-borne relapsing fever .**

**Some pathogens can live their entire lifecycle outside the host. These include threadworm and several faecal-oral bacteria which cause bacillary dysentery, (para)typhoid, and salmonellosis.**

**Animal hosts, asymptomatic carriers, and other potential reservoirs of pathogens can be important sources of infection, and this must be taken into account when trying to control disease. The whole population at risk may have to be treated, or animal hosts controlled. With several diseases these preventive measures will have to be maintained over a long period before a reduction in the occurrence of the infection will be noticeable.**

### *Transmission of disease*

**To survive as a species, pathogens must infect new people or animals. To do this, they must leave the body of the host, find their way to a new susceptible person or animal, and enter the body of that person or animal. As the exit, transmission, and entry of the pathogens are closely associated, we will cover them together.**

**Water and environmental sanitation interventions that aim to improve the health of a population usually try to reduce the risk of transmission of infection. To do this appropriately, the WES specialist needs to be familiar with the pathogens' transmission route(s). It is this understanding that enables the specialist to deter-mine which control measures will be most effective in a particular situation.**

**As many infections are linked to WES, it is useful to categorize the different diseases.**

## *CONTROLLING AND PREVENTING DISEASE*

**For a water and sanitation specialist the most useful categorization is based on the transmission cycles of the infections. Generally speaking, diseases with similar transmission cycles can be controlled by similar preventive measures, and will occur in similar environments.**

**The infections are categorised and their transmission routes described at the same time. More information on the transmission routes and potentially effective preventive measures of specific diseases can be found .**

**Some terms relating to the transmission or classification of infections are defined here:**

**Food-borne infections: infections which can be transmitted through eating food containing the pathogen.**

**Vector-borne infections: infections transmitted through vectors. We use vector-borne infections only for infections with a *biological vector*, that is a vector in which the pathogen goes through a development before further transmission is possible (e.g. mosquitoes, tsetse fly, body louse). We do not classify as vector-borne those infections which are transmitted by *mechanical vectors*, that is the animal is only a vehicle for transporting the pathogen (e.g. domestic flies, cockroaches).**

**Water-borne infections:** infections which can be transmitted through drinking-water which contains the pathogen.

**Water-washed infections:** infections caused by pathogens whose transmission can be prevented by improving personal hygiene.

Infections can have either direct or indirect transmission routes.

## Infections with direct transmission

A pathogen with a direct transmission route can infect a susceptible person or animal immediately after leaving the host. The pathogen does not need to develop in the environment, in an intermediate host, or in a vector.

In faecal pathogens these are the non-latent infectious agents.

This group contains three disease-groups: faeces-oral infections, lepidopterist, and infections spread through direct contact.

*DISEASE AND DISEASE TRANSMISSION*

***Faeces-oral infections***

**These pathogens leave the host through faeces, and enter the susceptible person or animal through ingestion. Transmission occurs mainly through direct contact with contaminated fingers; food contaminated directly with excreta, contaminated hands, domestic flies, soil, or water; contaminated drinking-water; or contaminant-nated soil. Faeces-oral infections are food-borne, water-borne, and water-washed. As faecal-oral infections are transmitted directly, any route that will take matter polluted with faeces directly or indirectly to somebody's mouth could potentially transmit the pathogen.**

## CONTROLLING AND PREVENTING DISEASE

*Leptospirosis*

**The main reservoir of lepidopterist is normally rats, though many other animals can potentially transmit the infection. The pathogen leaves the animal host through urine. People are usually infected through direct skin contact with water, moist soil, or vegetation contaminated with urine from infected animals. Other ways of transmission are direct contact with body tissues of infected animals or ingesting food contaminated with urine. Transmission from person to person is rare .**

*Infections of direct contact*

All the diseases covered in this manual that fall into this category are infections which affect the skin or eyes. Pathogens are present on the skin or in the discharges of affected body parts or eyes. The pathogens are transmitted directly through contaminated hands, clothes, domestic flies, or any other contaminated material.

The pathogen enters the body through skin or mucous membranes such as the eyes. These infections are associated with poor personal hygiene and are water-washed.

Few of these infections have animal hosts. The diseases in this category include conjunctivitis, trachoma, yaws, and scabies.

### Infections with indirect transmission

A pathogen with an indirect transmission route must go through a development phase outside the host before it can infect a new susceptible person or animal. This development will take place in a specific intermediate host, vector, or type of environment.

This need to go through a particular organism or environment gives the transmis-sion route a focus, which preventive measures can target, for example by vector control or improved food preparation.

In the fecal pathogens these are the latent infectious agents.

**The disease-groups with indirect transmission are soil-transmitted helminths, water-based helminths, beef/pork tapeworm infection, Guinea-worm infection, and vector-borne infections.**

## DISEASE AND DISEASE TRANSMISSION

*Soil-transmitted helminths*

**These worms leave the body through faeces as eggs or larvae. After excretion they have to develop in soil. They can be further divided based on how the pathogen enters the human body.**

**Entrance by penetration of the skin: the pathogen enters the body through skin which is in direct contact with contaminated soil. This is the method used by hookworms and threadworms.**

**Entrance by ingestion: if either contaminated soil, or food or hands contami-nated with polluted soil come into contact with the mouth, the pathogen can be transmitted. These infections can be food-borne and water-washed. This method is used by roundworms and whipworms.**

**The infections covered here do not have animal hosts. The transmission routes is the soil-transmitted helminths.**

*Water-based helminths*

**These pathogens leave the body through excreta. The infectious agents must develop in intermediate hosts living**

**in freshwater. The transmission of these infections is therefore only possible if excreta containing the pathogens reaches fresh surface water in which there are suitable intermediate host(s). Based on transmission cycle, this category can be sub-divided in two groups:**

**Schistosomiasis. After excretion, the pathogen infects a freshwater snail, in which it develops and multiplies. The snail releases the pathogens into the water, and people are infected when these pathogens penetrate skin which is in direct contact with infected freshwater. Only one type of schistosomiasis (which occurs only in Asia) has an important reservoir in an animal host; all other types have people as the only host of importance.**

**Water-based helminths with two water-based intermediate hosts. The first inter-mediate host is a freshwater snail or copepod. The second intermediate host is a freshwater plant, fish, or crabs/crayfish. The intermediate hosts are specific to the pathogen. These infections are food-borne and people become infected when they eat the second intermediate host without properly cooking it. All these infections affect both animals and people. These diseases include opisthorchiasis, clonorchiasis, and lung fluke disease.**

***Beef/pig tapeworm infection***

**The pathogens leave the person through faeces. The excreted eggs then have to be ingested by either cattle or**

**pigs. Once the pathogen is ingested by the animal, it will develop in the body of the cow or pig. The infections are food-borne and people become infected when they eat undercooked beef or pork containing the pathogen. People are the only hosts to the infection.**

**A dangerous complication called cysticercosis is possible when people ingest the eggs of the pig tapeworm. The pathogen will form cysts throughout the person's body. Transmission of this infection is like faecal-oral infections.**

*Guinea-worm*

**In this infection the pathogen, a large worm, creates a blister on the person's skin, which erupts when it comes into contact with water, releasing the worm's larvae. These larvae then infect a copepod (*Cyclops*), in which it develops. The disease is water-borne. People become infected by drinking water containing *Cyclops,* and are the only host to this infection.**

## *Vector-borne diseases*

**These infections are transmitted by vectors. Vectors are arthropods (insects, ticks, or mites) which can transmit infections from host to future host . The pathogen exists in the blood or skin of the host. The vector becomes infected when it feeds on a host. The pathogen develops and multiplies inside the vector, which then becomes infectious. People are usually infected through the bite of an infectious vector, though other ways of entry are possible. With several vector-borne dis-eases animal hosts are important reservoirs. Vector-borne diseases include yellow fever, malaria, sleeping sickness, plague, epidemic louse-borne typhus fever, and louse-borne relapsing fever.**

# DISEASE AND DISEASE TRANSMISSION

## The environment

The environment is everything that surrounds the pathogen in its transmission from host to susceptible person or animal. Obviously the environment is a vast subject, and we can only look at some of the more important environmental factors here.

Interventions which involve WES will often modify the environment to try to reduce the transmission risk.

The environmental factors that we will look at here are climate, landscape, human surroundings, and human behaviour. Environmental factors are often associated, for example higher altitudes result in lower temperatures, landscapes are formed by the climate.

## The climate

The climate and its seasonal changes play an important role in disease transmis-sion. The presence of vectors and intermediate hosts often depends on rain and temperature.

The hematological requirements of the vector or intermediate hosts can predict whether an infection is likely to be a problem in an area. Malaria, for example, will normally not occur in temperatures below 16°C and infection is thus unlikely at altitudes above 2,000 metres.

In general, direct sunlight, a dry environment, times of pathogens in the environment.

**Conditions may not be suitable to transmission year round, and many infections are seasonal, occurring when the environment is favourable to transmission. Mosquito-borne infections, like malaria and yellow fever, are linked to the rainy season. The occurrence of diarrhoeal diseases often increases with the first rains after the dry season, as faecal pollution is washed into rivers. Ponds which disappear in the dry season may in the wet season contain water with snails that will transmit schistosomiasis.**

**The climate influences human behaviour. In cold climates people will crowd together and wear more clothing. If this is combined with poor personal hygiene the the body-louse, vector of louse-borne typhus fever and louse-borne relapsing fever, can thrive.**

In warmer climates children are also likely to play in surface water, where they can be infected with schistosomiasis.

## The landscape

The landscape consists of the larger physical structures in the environment. These structures are usually natural, but can be man-made. They include mountains, deserts, rivers, jungle, artificial water reservoirs, and deforested areas. Aspects of the landscape that would influence disease transmission most are the micro-climate, the presence of water, and types of vegetation.

Man-made modifications of the landscape often increase the risk of disease transmission by creating a habitat favourable to vectors or intermediate hosts. Large artificial water reservoirs frequently increase the occurrence of malaria and schistosomiasis (6), for example, and introducing irrigation schemes can increase the occurrence of schistosomiasis (15).

Although the WES specialist working in the field must recognise the risk-factors linked to the landscape, he or she will normally not be able to modify the landscape to reduce the risks of disease transmission.

**The human surroundings**

**Landscape and human surroundings are closely linked, and it is difficult to divide the two clearly. The difference is one of scale; while the landscape normally cannot be modified or improved by individual people, individuals can modify the human surroundings.**

**Although the landscape will normally be similar for all people living in an area, the human surroundings may be very different for people living in the same region, village, or even household. Many infections are linked to specific circum-stances, and people with specific occupations, socio-economic status, gender, or religion may be far more at risk than others. While the father of an African family may be exposed to leptospirosis and plague because he works in sugarcane fields and regularly traps rats, the mother may be exposed to sleeping sickness as she goes to the river to wash clothes, and the children may be exposed to schisto-somiasis while playing in the local pond.**

**The human surroundings are created by a combination of natural elements and how people have modified these elements.**

**People adapt their surroundings to their needs. If these adaptations are well done, they can help to prevent the transmission of disease. In practise they often**

## DISEASE AND DISEASE TRANSMISSION

Encourage the transmission of disease, however, as people do not have the space, motivation, understanding, time, energy, or financial or material means to do them properly.

In relation to the WES aspects, human surroundings are concerned with water supply, proper handling of excreta, removal of unwanted water, adequate management of solid waste, and control of vectors or intermediate hosts through modification of the environment or change in behaviour.

Waste products like excreta, wastewater, and refuse are disposed of in the human surroundings. These wastes must be properly managed to prevent them becoming a health risk.

The WES specialist working in the field will have to know what aspects of the human surroundings increase the risk of disease transmission. This will enable him or her to determine which aspects play an important role in the transmission of disease in a specific situation. Based on this, an intervention can be planned which will reduce the health risks to the population.

### Human behaviour

People behave in a certain way because they believe that they are making the most of their lives. Human behaviour

**is complex. It is influenced by culture, for example religion, attitudes, and traditional beliefs; by social position, such as gender or age; by availability of means, for example money, energy, time, or material; and by politics.**

**One type of hand pump may be acceptable in one culture, but unacceptable in another. One type of latrine may be preferred by men, while women or children might prefer another. People may not accept things from a government they despise, or from an insulting development worker.**

**Having access to a safe water supply, or technically adequate sanitation, does not automatically mean people will use them [25]. If people do not regard structures as acceptable, appropriate, or as an improvement to their quality of life, they will not be used, or will not be used to their full potential.**

**Interventions that have only focused on structural improvements have often given poor results in controlling infections. Studies in disease prevention indicate that the most important factor in reducing the transmission of diseases related to WES**

## CONTROLLING AND PREVENTING DISEASE

**Changing human behaviour in relation to WES should therefore be one of the priorities of the WES specialist.**

**The specialist will have to identify existing behaviour, attitudes, and behaviour concerning WES and their**

causes. This will form a base from which health and hygiene promotion can be introduced. All interventions should look at human behaviour, and where needed, reinforce existing positive behaviour while trying to modify behaviour that favours disease transmission.

## The future host

The success of a pathogen in infecting a person will depend on:

(i)the infectious dose of the pathogen, and the number of infectious agents which manage to enter the potential new host (this applies mainly to faecal-oral infections); and
(ii)whether the pathogen can overcome the barriers of the host.

These two factors are now considered in more detail.

## The infectious dose

The infectious dose is the number of pathogens which have to enter the body of a susceptible person to cause infection. Although this figure should not be seen as exact, it does give an indication of how easily an infection can occur.

The infectious dose is normally only used for faecal-oral infections. As every larva of a helminth can become an adult worm, worms have a very low infectious dose. Infections with a low infectious dose are more likely to be spread by direct person-to-person contact than infections with a high infectious dose. Measures such as improving drinking-water quality, or reducing the concentration of

**pathogens in surface water (for exampleby treating sewage), are more likely to have effect on infections with high infectious doses than on those with low ones. Intuitively one would say that flies are more likely to transmit infections with a low infec-tious dose, but this is complicated by the fact that several bacteria can multiply in food, and thus reach the infectious dose in this way.**

# DISEASE AND DISEASE TRANSMISSION

## The barriers of the body against pathogens

**The body has a range of mechanisms that prevent a pathogen from causing infection.**

**The skin and mucous membranes have anti-microbial substances, and the stom-ach is acid to act as the first barriers against pathogens. Low acidity in the stomach or an open wound (e.g. insect bite, cut, abrasion) can make this barrier ineffective.**

**The next barriers are mechanisms that react to the pathogen, and try to counter its development. These barriers are not specific to the pathogen, and the body does not need to have been in contact with the pathogen for them to be effective. These mechanisms are the host's resistance against pathogens . Resistance is lowered if someone is suffering from other infections , or is malnourished, stressed, or fatigued . Women have a higher risk of infection when pregnant .**

**An individual's immune system may have experienced a pathogen through an earlier infection or immunization (vaccination) with inactivated pathogens. When the pathogens enter the person's body, their immune system will recognize the pathogen and make antibodies which will attack the pathogen. This is called active immunity . The effectiveness of active immunity depends on the pathogen, and the length of time since the body has been in**

contact with the pathogen. Active immunity is effective only against that particular pathogen. The effectiveness against bacteria and viruses usually lasts for years .

Passive immunity is created by introducing foreign antibodies into the body. An unborn baby receives antibodies from the mother through the placenta, which will protect it for some time after birth. Vaccination with antibodies is another way of creating passive immunity. The foreign antibodies will slowly disappear from the body, and passive immunity will usually only last days or months .

## CONTROLLING AND PREVENTING DISEASE

A person or animal who lacks effective barriers (has a poor resistance and/or a low immunity) against a pathogen is susceptible to this infectious agent .

Two important practical points define the susceptibility of a population:

*A population that is weakened because of poor nutrition or a high occurrence of disease, fatigue, or stress has an increased risk of disease.
*When a pathogen is very common in a population, or the population is immunised, most people will have some form of immunity against it. In this case the disease will attack mainly children. If the same pathogen is introduced into a

population which has low immunity, there is a risk of an outbreak (an epidemic) which can attack all ages.

The infection over time

When a pathogen is introduced in sufficient numbers, and overcomes the resist-ace and immune system of a person or animal, infection will follow. The time between entrance of pathogen and appearance of the first signs of disease or symptoms is called the incubation period. As mentioned earlier, not all infections will result in disease, and for many infections asymptomatic carriers are common.



## VIRUS:

**Virus is the microorganisms which have the properties of living and non-living both. They have a specific structure which consists of head and tail. Head is composed of several protein units known as capsomeres which enclose the genetic material made up of RNA or DNA. They have a lipid envelope derived from the host cell membrane which lies outside the capsomere. They occur in crystalline form**

**outside the body of the host but as it enters the host cell ,it injects its genetic material which replicates vigorously. The replicated materials are further packed in the new protein coat formed using host protein and is thrown out by the destruction of cell membrane.**

## ***ORIGIN OF VIRUS:***

***Microbiologists have shown that*** **virus family concept is fundamentally important in understanding the biologic classification of viruses based on following criteria:**

**(i) By specifying the family to which a virus belongs, much can be inferred about its physical, chemical, and biologic properties and its evolutionary relationships and modes of gene expression.**

**(ii) Virus families are designated with the suffix -viridae.**

**(iii) Families are distinguished largely on the basis of physiochemical properties, genome structure, size, morphology, and molecular processes.**

**(iv) There are different criteria that are used to differentiate human virus families.**

**There are different criteria for the classifications of VIRUS FAMILIES:**

**(i)Criteria for type of genomics nucleic acid and strandedness is done on the basis of DNA or RNA**

**(ii) Criteria for Nucleic acid is done for the ds, ss, partially ds**

**(iii) Criteria of Sense of ss nucleic acid is done on the basis of +, −, − with ambisense**

**(iv) Criteria for the Capsid morphology is done on the basis of Icosahedral, helical, or complex.**

**(v) Criteria of Envelope is done on the basis of Present or absent.**

**(vi) Criteria for the Genome segmentation is done on the basis of Number of segments.**

**(vii) Criteria for the Genomic structure is done on the basis of For example, type of RNA cap, location of structural genes or repeat sequences**

**(vii) Critera for the Size of virion and/or genome is done on the basis of For example, large-genome DNA viruses (e.g., poxviruses, herpesviruses) versus small-genome viruses (e.g., picornaviruses, parvoviruses, hepadnaviruses).**

**(viii) Criteria for the Nature of gene expression, including nature and number of mRNA transcripts is done on the basis of For example, use of genomic polyproteins (e.g.,**

**picornaviruses, flaviviruses); use of reverse transcriptase (e.g., retroviruses, hepadnaviruses); use of multiple 3′ nested genes (e.g., coronaviruses); use of RNA ambisense coding (e.g., arenaviruses, bunyaviruses.ds, double stranded; ss, single stranded.**

**(ix) Criteria for the Electron micrographic (EM) appearance is done on the basis of For example, bullet-shaped rhabdoviruses or star-shaped astroviruses**

***The 26 virus families implicated in human disease.They are given below . In some cases, humans serve as a reservoir for the viruses and the link to human disease is clear. In other cases, humans may be incidental hosts or the link to disease may be more tenuous. We list specific viruses within each family that are linked to human disease.(WHO DATA)***

# Human Viral Infections are Listed by Family[a]

**WHO DATA**

| | |
|---|---|
| *Paramyxoviridae* | *Measles (rubeola) virus, mumps virus, parainfluenza viruses, Hendra virus, Nipah virus, Menangle virus*[38] |
| *Parvoviridae* | *Human parvovirus B19, human bocavirus,*[39] *adeno-associated viruses*[c], [e] |
| *Picobirnaviridae* | *Human picobirnavirus* |
| *Picornaviridae*[40] | *Genus Enterovirus: human rhinoviruses (>100 serotypes), enteroviruses (>100 serotypes, including poliovirus 1–3, coxsackievirus A and B, echoviruses, and other human enteroviruses)*<br>*Genus Hepatovirus: hepatitis A virus (HAV)*<br>*Genus Parechovirus: human parechoviruses*<br>*Genus Kobuvirus: Aichi virus*<br>*Genus Cosavirus: human cosaviruses*[41]<br>*Genus Cardiovirus: Vilyuisk human encephalomyelitis virus, Saffold viruses*[42]<br>*Genus Salivirus: human klassevirus,*[43] *salivirus A*<br>*Genus Senecavirus: Seneca Valley virus*[f]<br>*Unassigned: Syr-Darya Valley fever virus* |
| *Pneumoviridae* | *Respiratory syncytial virus, human metapneumoviruses* |
| *Polyomaviridae* | *JC virus, BK virus, KI virus, WU virus, Merkel cell polyomavirus, lymphotropic polyomavirus, human* |

| | |
|---|---|
| | *polyomavirus 6, human polyomavirus 7, trichodysplasia spinulosa-associated polyomavirus, human polyomavirus 9*[44, 45] |
| *Poxviridae* | *Molluscum contagiosum virus, variola (smallpox) virus, monkeypox virus, vaccinia virus, orf virus, pseudocowpox virus, Tanapox virus, Yaba monkey tumor virus*[46] |
| *Reoviridae* | *Human rotavirus, Colorado tick fever virus, human reovirus,*[c] *Kemerovo virus* |
| *Retroviridae* | *Human immunodeficiency viruses types 1 and 2, human T-lymphocyte lymphotropic viruses,*[47] *xenotropic murine leukemia virus-related virus,*[g] *human endogenous retroviruses (HERVs), simian foamy virus* |
| *Rhabdoviridae* | *Rabies virus, vesicular stomatitis virus, Australian bat lyssavirus, Duvenhage virus, Mokola virus* |
| *Togaviridae* | *Rubella virus; Chikungunya virus; eastern equine, western equine, and Venezuelan equine encephalitis viruses; Ross River, Sindbis, and Semliki Forest viruses* |
| *Delta*[h] | *Hepatitis delta virus*[e] *(HDV)* |

*Common Routes of Virus Transmission to Humans are classified as follows:*

*(i) Respiratory route (i.e., droplet, aerosol, and respiratory secretions on the hands and elsewhere; oral exchange): influenza virus, varicella-zoster virus, human rhinovirus, human adenovirus, respiratory syncytial virus, parainfluenza virus, metapneumovirus*

*(ii) Fecal-oral route: polioviruses, coxsackieviruses, hepatitis A virus, rotavirus, astrovirus, norovirus*

*(iii) Direct contact: human papillomavirus (HPV), molluscum contagiosum, herpes simplex virus type 1 (HSV-1)*

*(iv) Sexual: human immunodeficiency virus type 1 (HIV-1), human T-lymphotropic virus type 1 (HTLV-1), hepatitis B virus (HBV), human papillomavirus types 16 and 18 (HPV-16, HPV18), HSV-2*

*(v) Urine-associated: cytomegalovirus (CMV)*

*(vi) Parenteral route (i.e., blood and blood products, transplantation, tattooing, and scarification): HIV-1, HBV, hepatitis C virus (HCV)*

*(vii) Animal bite: rabies virus, Duvenhage virus*

*(viii) Vertical route (e.g., germline, intrauterine, perinatal, human milk): HIV-1, HTLV-1, germline transmission of endogenous retroviruses*

*(ix) Arthropod-borne route (e.g., mosquitos, ticks, sandflies): Japanese encephalitis virus, West Nile virus, dengue virus, yellow fever virus, Zika virus, chikungunya virus, and many others*

*(x) Rodent-associated transmission: Lassa fever virus, sin nombre, and other hanta viruses (e.g., Hantaan virus, Seoul virus, and Puumala virus)*

*Bat-associated transmission: rabies virus, Nipah virus, Ebola virus, severe acute*


*11.Zarafshan Shiraz : Covid-19 Result of attempt to manufacture to AIDS Virus ? Nobel winning Scientist Sparks New Controversy.: 2020:India.com/Viral/Covid-19.*

*1. 26, 2020.*

*2. Antonio Regalado(2018). Exclusive:Chinese Scientists are creating CRISPR*
*babes :NATURE:BIOTECHNOLOGY:CRISPR.*

(xi) respiratory syndrome coronavirus (SARS CoV)

## DISEASE AND DISEASE TRANSMISSION

### Faeces-oral infections

These pathogens leave the host through faeces, and enter the susceptible person or animal through ingestion. Transmission occurs mainly through direct contact with contaminated fingers; food contaminated directly with excreta, contaminated hands, domestic flies, soil, or water; contaminated drinking-water; or contaminant-nated soil. Faeces-oral infections are food-borne, water-borne, and water-washed. As faecal-oral infections are transmitted directly, any route that will take matter polluted with faeces directly or indirectly to somebody's mouth could potentially transmit the pathogen.

## CONTROLLING AND PREVENTING DISEASE

### Leptospirosis

The main reservoir of lepidopterist is normally rats, though many other animals can potentially transmit the infection. The pathogen leaves the animal host through urine. People are usually infected through direct skin contact with water, moist soil, or vegetation contaminated with urine from infected animals. Other ways of transmission are direct contact with body tissues of infected animals or ingesting food contaminated with urine. Transmission from person to person is rare .

### *Infections of direct contact*

All the diseases covered in this manual that fall into this category are infections which affect the skin or eyes. Pathogens are present on the skin or in the discharges of affected body parts or eyes. The pathogens are transmitted directly through contaminated hands, clothes, domestic flies, or any other contaminated material.

The pathogen enters the body through skin or mucous membranes such as the eyes. These infections are associated with poor personal hygiene and are water-washed.

Few of these infections have animal hosts. The diseases in this category include conjunctivitis, trachoma, yaws, and scabies.

## Infections with indirect transmission

**A pathogen with an indirect transmission route must go through a development phase outside the host before it can infect a new susceptible person or animal. This development will take place in a specific intermediate host, vector, or type of environment.**

**This need to go through a particular organism or environment gives the transmis-sion route a focus, which preventive measures can target, for example by vector control or improved food preparation.**

**In the fecal pathogens these are the latent infectious agents.**

**The disease-groups with indirect transmission are soil-transmitted helminths, water-based**

**helminths, beef/pork tapeworm infection, Guinea-worm infection, and vector-borne infections.**

## DISEASE AND DISEASE TRANSMISSION

### *Soil-transmitted helminths*

**These worms leave the body through faeces as eggs or larvae. After excretion they have to develop in soil. They can be further divided based on how the pathogen enters the human body.**

**Entrance by penetration of the skin: the pathogen enters the body through skin which is in direct contact with contaminated soil. This is the method used by hookworms and threadworms.**

**Entrance by ingestion: if either contaminated soil, or food or hands contami-nated with polluted soil come into contact with the mouth, the pathogen can be transmitted. These infections can be food-borne and water-washed. This method is used by roundworms and whipworms.**

**The infections covered here do not have animal hosts. The transmission routes is the soil-transmitted helminths.**

*Water-based helminths*

**These pathogens leave the body through excreta. The infectious agents must develop in intermediate hosts living in freshwater. The transmission of these infections is therefore only possible if excreta containing the pathogens reaches fresh surface water in which there are suitable intermediate host(s). Based on transmission cycle, this category can be sub-divided in two groups:**

**Schistosomiasis. After excretion, the pathogen infects a freshwater snail, in which it develops and multiplies. The snail releases the pathogens into the water, and people are infected when these pathogens penetrate skin which is in direct contact with infected freshwater. Only one type of schistosomiasis (which occurs only in Asia) has an important reservoir in an animal host; all other types have people as the only host of importance.**

**Water-based helminths with two water-based intermediate hosts. The first inter-mediate host is a freshwater snail or**

**copepod. The second intermediate host is a freshwater plant, fish, or crabs/crayfish. The intermediate hosts are specific to the pathogen. These infections are food-borne and people become infected when they eat the second intermediate host without properly cooking it. All these infections affect both animals and people. These diseases include opisthorchiasis, clonorchiasis, and lung fluke disease.**

### *Beef/pig tapeworm infection*

**The pathogens leave the person through faeces. The excreted eggs then have to be ingested by either cattle or pigs. Once the pathogen is ingested by the animal, it will develop in the body of the cow or pig. The infections are food-borne and people become infected when they eat undercooked beef or pork containing the pathogen. People are the only hosts to the infection.**

**A dangerous complication called cysticercosis is possible when people ingest the eggs of the pig tapeworm. The pathogen will form cysts throughout the person's body. Transmission of this infection is like faecal-oral infections.**

### *Guinea-worm*

**In this infection the pathogen, a large worm, creates a blister on the person's skin, which erupts when it comes into contact with water, releasing the worm's larvae. These larvae then infect a copepod (*Cyclops*), in which it develops. The disease is water-borne. People become infected by drinking water containing *Cyclops,* and are the only host to this infection.**

*Vector-borne diseases*

**These infections are transmitted by vectors. Vectors are arthropods (insects, ticks, or mites) which can transmit infections from host to future host . The pathogen exists in the blood or skin of the host. The vector becomes infected when it feeds on a host. The pathogen develops and multiplies inside the vector, which then becomes infectious. People are usually infected through the bite of an infectious vector, though other ways of entry are possible. With several vector-borne dis-eases animal hosts are important reservoirs. Vector-borne diseases include yellow fever, malaria, sleeping sickness, plague, epidemic louse-borne typhus fever, and louse-borne relapsing fever.**

# DISEASE AND DISEASE TRANSMISSION

## The environment

**The environment is everything that surrounds the pathogen in its transmission from host to susceptible person or animal. Obviously the environment is a vast subject, and we can only look at some of the more important environmental factors here.**

**Interventions which involve WES will often modify the environment to try to reduce the transmission risk.**

**The environmental factors that we will look at here are climate, landscape, human surroundings, and human behaviour. Environmental factors are often associated, for example higher altitudes result in lower temperatures, landscapes are formed by the climate.**

## The climate

**The climate and its seasonal changes play an important role in disease transmis-sion. The presence of vectors and intermediate hosts often depends on rain and temperature.**

**The hematological requirements of the vector or intermediate hosts can predict whether an infection is**

likely to be a problem in an area. Malaria, for example, will normally not occur in temperatures below 16°C and infection is thus unlikely at altitudes above 2,000 metres.

In general, direct sunlight, a dry environment, and high temperatures will reduce the survival times of pathogens in the environment.

Conditions may not be suitable to transmission year round, and many infections are seasonal, occurring when the environment is favourable to transmission. Mosquito-borne infections, like malaria and yellow fever, are linked to the rainy season. The occurrence of diarrhoeal diseases often increases with the first rains after the dry season, as faecal pollution is washed into rivers. Ponds which disappear in the dry season may in the wet season contain water with snails that will transmit schistosomiasis.

The climate influences human behaviour. In cold climates people will crowd together and wear more clothing. If this is combined with poor personal hygiene the the body-louse, vector of louse-borne typhus fever and louse-borne relapsing fever, can thrive.

**In warmer climates children are also likely to play in surface water, where they can be infected with schistosomiasis.**

## The landscape

**The landscape consists of the larger physical structures in the environment. These structures are usually natural, but can be man-made. They include mountains, deserts, rivers, jungle, artificial water reservoirs, and deforested areas. Aspects of the landscape that would influence disease transmission most are the micro-climate, the presence of water, and types of vegetation.**

**Man-made modifications of the landscape often increase the risk of disease transmission by creating a habitat favourable to vectors or intermediate hosts. Large artificial water reservoirs frequently increase the occurrence of malaria and schistosomiasis [(6)], for example, and introducing irrigation schemes can increase the occurrence of schistosomiasis [(15)].**

**Although the WES specialist working in the field must recognise the risk-factors linked to the landscape, he or she will normally not be able to modify the landscape to reduce the risks of disease transmission.**

## The human surroundings

**Landscape and human surroundings are closely linked, and it is difficult to divide the two clearly. The difference is one of scale; while the landscape normally cannot be modified or improved by individual people, individuals can modify the human surroundings.**

**Although the landscape will normally be similar for all people living in an area, the human surroundings may be very different for people living in the same region, village, or even household. Many infections are linked to specific circum-stances, and people with specific occupations, socio-economic status, gender, or religion may be far more at risk than others. While the father of an African family may be exposed to leptospirosis and plague because he works in sugarcane fields and regularly traps rats, the mother may be exposed to sleeping sickness as she goes to the river to wash clothes, and the children may be exposed to schisto-somiasis while playing in the local pond.**

**The human surroundings are created by a combination of natural elements and how people have modified these elements.**

**People adapt their surroundings to their needs. If these adaptations are well done, they can help to prevent the transmission of disease. In practise they often**

## DISEASE AND DISEASE TRANSMISSION

**Encourage the transmission of disease, however, as people do not have the space, motivation, understanding, time, energy, or financial or material means to do them properly.**

**In relation to the WES aspects, human surroundings are concerned with water supply, proper handling of excreta, removal of unwanted water, adequate management of solid waste, and control of vectors or intermediate hosts through modification of the environment or change in behaviour.**

**Waste products like excreta, wastewater, and refuse are disposed of in the human surroundings. These wastes must be properly managed to prevent them becoming a health risk.**

**The WES specialist working in the field will have to know what aspects of the human surroundings increase the risk of disease transmission. This will enable him or her to determine which aspects play an important role in the transmission of disease in a specific situation. Based on**

this, an intervention can be planned which will reduce the health risks to the population.

## Human behaviour

People behave in a certain way because they believe that they are making the most of their lives. Human behaviour is complex. It is influenced by culture, for example religion, attitudes, and traditional beliefs; by social position, such as gender or age; by availability of means, for example money, energy, time, or material; and by politics.

One type of hand pump may be acceptable in one culture, but unacceptable in another. One type of latrine may be preferred by men, while women or children might prefer another. People may not accept things from a government they despise, or from an insulting development worker.

Having access to a safe water supply, or technically adequate sanitation, does not automatically mean people will use them [(25)]. If people do not regard structures as acceptable, appropriate, or as an improvement to their quality of life, they will not be used, or will not be used to their full potential.

**Interventions that have only focused on structural improvements have often given poor results in controlling infections. Studies in disease prevention indicate that the most important factor in reducing the transmission of diseases related to WES**

## CONTROLLING AND PREVENTING DISEASE

**Changing human behaviour in relation to WES should therefore be one of the priorities of the WES specialist.**

**The specialist will have to identify existing behaviour, attitudes, and behaviour concerning WES and their causes. This will form a base from which health and hygiene promotion can be introduced. All interventions should look at human behaviour, and where needed, reinforce existing positive behaviour while trying to modify behaviour that favours disease transmission.**

## The future host

**The success of a pathogen in infecting a person will depend on:**

(i)the infectious dose of the pathogen, and the number of infectious agents which manage to enter the potential new host (this applies mainly to faecal-oral infections); and

(ii)whether the pathogen can overcome the barriers of the host.

These two factors are now considered in more detail.

## The infectious dose

The infectious dose is the number of pathogens which have to enter the body of a susceptible person to cause infection. Although this figure should not be seen as exact, it does give an indication of how easily an infection can occur.

The infectious dose is normally only used for faecal-oral infections. As every larva of a helminth can become an adult worm, worms have a very low infectious dose.

Infections with a low infectious dose are more likely to be spread by direct person-to-person contact than infections with a high infectious dose. Measures such as improving drinking-water quality, or reducing the concentration of pathogens in surface water (for exampleby treating sewage), are more likely to have effect on infections with high infectious doses than on those with low ones. Intuitively one would say that flies are more likely to transmit infections with a low infec-tious dose, but this is

**complicated by the fact that several bacteria can multiply in food, and thus reach the infectious dose in this way.**

# DISEASE AND DISEASE TRANSMISSION

## The barriers of the body against pathogens

**The body has a range of mechanisms that prevent a pathogen from causing infection.**

**The skin and mucous membranes have anti-microbial substances, and the stom-ach is acid to act as the first barriers against pathogens. Low acidity in the stomach or an open wound (e.g. insect bite, cut, abrasion) can make this barrier ineffective.**

**The next barriers are mechanisms that react to the pathogen, and try to counter its development. These barriers are not specific to the pathogen, and the body does not need to have been in contact with the pathogen for them to be effective. These mechanisms are the host's resistance against pathogens . Resistance is lowered if someone is suffering from other infections , or is malnourished, stressed, or fatigued . Women have a higher risk of infection when pregnant .**

**An individual's immune system may have experienced a pathogen through an earlier infection or immunization**

(vaccination) with inactivated pathogens. When the pathogens enter the person's body, their immune system will recognize the pathogen and make antibodies which will attack the pathogen. This is called active immunity. The effectiveness of active immunity depends on the pathogen, and the length of time since the body has been in contact with the pathogen. Active immunity is effective only against that particular pathogen. The effectiveness against bacteria and viruses usually lasts for years.

Passive immunity is created by introducing foreign antibodies into the body. An unborn baby receives antibodies from the mother through the placenta, which will protect it for some time after birth. Vaccination with antibodies is another way of creating passive immunity. The foreign antibodies will slowly disappear from the body, and passive immunity will usually only last days or months.

## CONTROLLING AND PREVENTING DISEASE

A person or animal who lacks effective barriers (has a poor resistance and/or a low immunity) against a pathogen is susceptible to this infectious agent.

**Two important practical points define the susceptibility of a population:**

***A population that is weakened because of poor nutrition or a high occurrence of disease, fatigue, or stress has an increased risk of disease.**

***When a pathogen is very common in a population, or the population is immunised, most people will have some form of immunity against it. In this case the disease will attack mainly children. If the same pathogen is introduced into a population which has low immunity, there is a risk of an outbreak (an epidemic) which can attack all ages.**

## The infection over time

**When a pathogen is introduced in sufficient numbers, and overcomes the resist-ace and immune system of a person or animal, infection will follow. The time between entrance of pathogen and appearance of the first signs of disease or symptoms is called the incubation period. As mentioned earlier, not all infections will result in disease, and for many infections asymptomatic carriers are common.**

## VIRUS:

**Virus is the microorganisms which have the properties of living and non-living both. They have a specific structure which consists of head and tail. Head is composed of several protein units known as capsomeres which enclose the genetic material made up of RNA or DNA. They have a lipid envelope derived from the host cell membrane which lies outside the capsomere. They occur in crystalline form outside the body of the host but as it enters the host cell ,it injects its genetic material which replicates vigorously. The replicated materials are further packed in the new protein coat formed using host protein and is thrown out by the destruction of cell membrane.**

## *ORIGIN OF VIRUS:*

*Microbiologists have shown that* **virus family concept is fundamentally important in understanding the biologic classification of viruses based on following criteria:**

**(i) By specifying the family to which a virus belongs, much can be inferred about its physical, chemical, and biologic properties and its evolutionary relationships and modes of gene expression.**

**(ii) Virus families are designated with the suffix -viridae.**

**(iii) Families are distinguished largely on the basis of physiochemical properties, genome structure, size, morphology, and molecular processes.**

**(iv) There are different criteria that are used to differentiate human virus families.**

**There are different criteria for the classifications of VIRUS FAMILIES:**

**(i)Criteria for type of genomics nucleic acid and strandedness is done on the basis of DNA or RNA**

**(ii) Criteria for Nucleic acid is done for the ds, ss, partially ds**

**(iii) Criteria of Sense of ss nucleic acid is done on the basis of +, −, − with ambisense**

**(iv) Criteria for the Capsid morphology is done on the basis of Icosahedral, helical, or complex.**

**(v) Criteria of Envelope is done on the basis of Present or absent.**

**(vi) Criteria for the Genome segmentation is done on the basis of Number of segments.**

**(vii) Criteria for the Genomic structure is done on the basis of For example, type of RNA cap, location of structural genes or repeat sequences**

**(vii) Critera for the Size of virion and/or genome is done on the basis of For example, large-genome DNA viruses (e.g., poxviruses, herpesviruses) versus small-genome viruses (e.g., picornaviruses, parvoviruses, hepadnaviruses).**

**(viii) Criteria for the Nature of gene expression, including nature and number of mRNA transcripts is done on the basis of For example, use of genomic polyproteins (e.g., picornaviruses, flaviviruses); use of reverse transcriptase (e.g., retroviruses, hepadnaviruses); use of multiple 3′ nested genes (e.g., coronaviruses); use of RNA ambisense coding (e.g., arenaviruses, bunyaviruses.ds, double stranded; ss, single stranded.**

**(ix) Criteria for the Electron micrographic (EM) appearance is done on the basis of For example, bullet-shaped rhabdoviruses or star-shaped astroviruses**

*The 26 virus families implicated in human disease.They are given below . In some cases, humans serve as a reservoir for the viruses and the link to human disease is clear. In other cases, humans may be incidental hosts or the link to disease may be more tenuous. We list specific viruses within each family that are linked to human disease.(WHO DATA)*

**Human Viral Infections are Listed by Family[a] WHO DATA**

| | |
|---|---|
| *Paramyxoviridae* | *Measles (rubeola) virus, mumps virus, parainfluenza viruses, Hendra virus, Nipah virus, Menangle virus*38 |
| *Parvoviridae* | *Human parvovirus B19, human bocavirus,*39 *adeno-associated viruses*[c], [e] |
| *Picobirnaviridae* | *Human picobirnavirus* |
| *Picornaviridae*40 | *Genus Enterovirus: human rhinoviruses (>100 serotypes), enteroviruses (>100 serotypes, including poliovirus 1–3, coxsackievirus A and B, echoviruses, and other human enteroviruses)*<br>*Genus Hepatovirus: hepatitis A virus (HAV)*<br>*Genus Parechovirus: human parechoviruses*<br>*Genus Kobuvirus: Aichi virus*<br>*Genus Cosavirus: human cosaviruses*41<br>*Genus Cardiovirus: Vilyuisk human encephalomyelitis virus, Saffold viruses*42 |

| | |
|---|---|
| | ***Genus Salivirus: human klassevirus,[43] salivirus A Genus Senecavirus: Seneca Valley virus[f] Unassigned: Syr-Darya Valley fever virus*** |
| *Pneumoviridae* | *Respiratory syncytial virus, human metapneumoviruses* |
| *Polyomaviridae* | *JC virus, BK virus, KI virus, WU virus, Merkel cell polyomavirus, lymphotropic polyomavirus, human polyomavirus 6, human polyomavirus 7, trichodysplasia spinulosa-associated polyomavirus, human polyomavirus 9*[44, 45] |
| *Poxviridae* | *Molluscum contagiosum virus, variola (smallpox) virus, monkeypox virus, vaccinia virus, orf virus, pseudocowpox virus, Tanapox virus, Yaba monkey tumor virus*[46] |
| *Reoviridae* | *Human rotavirus, Colorado tick fever virus, human reovirus,*[c] *Kemerovo virus* |
| *Retroviridae* | *Human immunodeficiency viruses types 1 and 2, human T-lymphocyte lymphotropic viruses,*[47] *xenotropic murine leukemia virus-related* |

| | |
|---|---|
| | *virus,[g] human endogenous retroviruses (HERVs), simian foamy virus* |
| *Rhabdoviridae* | *Rabies virus, vesicular stomatitis virus, Australian bat lyssavirus, Duvenhage virus, Mokola virus* |
| *Togaviridae* | *Rubella virus; Chikungunya virus; eastern equine, western equine, and Venezuelan equine encephalitis viruses; Ross River, Sindbis, and Semliki Forest viruses* |
| *Delta[h]* | *Hepatitis delta virus[e] (HDV)* |

*Common Routes of Virus Transmission to Humans are classified as follows:*

*(i) Respiratory route (i.e., droplet, aerosol, and respiratory secretions on the hands and elsewhere; oral exchange): influenza virus, varicella-zoster virus, human rhinovirus, human adenovirus, respiratory syncytial virus, parainfluenza virus, metapneumovirus*
*(ii) Fecal-oral route: polioviruses, coxsackieviruses, hepatitis A virus, rotavirus, astrovirus, norovirus*
*(iii) Direct contact: human papillomavirus (HPV), molluscum contagiosum, herpes simplex virus type 1 (HSV-1)*
*(iv) Sexual: human immunodeficiency virus type 1 (HIV-1), human T-lymphotropic virus type 1 (HTLV-1), hepatitis B virus (HBV), human papillomavirus types 16 and 18 (HPV-16, HPV18), HSV-2*
*(v) Urine-associated: cytomegalovirus (CMV)*

*(vi) Parenteral route (i.e., blood and blood products, transplantation, tattooing, and scarification): HIV-1, HBV, hepatitis C virus (HCV)*
*(vii) Animal bite: rabies virus, Duvenhage virus*
*(viii) Vertical route (e.g., germline, intrauterine, perinatal, human milk): HIV-1, HTLV-1, germline transmission of endogenous retroviruses*
*(ix) Arthropod-borne route (e.g., mosquitos, ticks, sandflies): Japanese encephalitis virus, West Nile virus, dengue virus, yellow fever virus, Zika virus, chikungunya virus, and many others*
*(x) Rodent-associated transmission: Lassa fever virus, sin nombre, and other hanta viruses (e.g., Hantaan virus, Seoul virus, and Puumala virus)*
*(xi) Bat-associated transmission: rabies virus, Nipah virus, Ebola virus, severe acute respiratory syndrome coronavirus (SARS CoV)*
*(xii) Monkey-associated transmission: herpes B virus, monkeypox virus, orf virus*
*(xiii) Other zoonotic associations (e.g., cows, sheep): orf virus, cowpox virus*

*Understanding virus classification can lead tort ant generalizations regarding the prevention.*

***Instead, viruses and bacteria both descended from an ancient cellular life form (CFL). But while – like humans – bacteria evolved to become more complex, viruses became simpler.***

***Today, viruses are so small and simple, they can't even replicate on their own. Viruses carry only the essential genetic information they need to be able to slip inside a host cell and coax it into making new copies of the virus. The influenza virus, for instance, has a mere 14 protein-coding genes. Because viruses are usually so basic, many biologists didn't think they could even be classified as a life form.***

**There are three main theories for the origin of virus.**

**(i) Biologists have studied and found that viruses are more ancient than the cellular organisms and predate the 'Last Universal Common Ancestor' (LUCA). This theory implies that ancient viruses had the ability to self-sustain and replicate on their own . This theory has received a fair amount of criticism because all modern day viruses need a cellular host to replicate and follow a parasitic life cycle .**

## (ii) The reduction hypothesis

**This theory states that viruses are degenerates (reduced forms) of modern day parasitic organisms and evolved by reductive evolutionary processes. In doing so, they lost all the genes required for self-sustenance (e.g., metabolic genes) and maintained only those required to parasite the host cells .**

**The reduction hypothesis has been preferred on grounds of lack of intermediates between viruses and parasitic organisms . Recently, giant viruses (e.g., mini viruses and mega viruses) have been shown to cross the barriers between viruses and small parasitic organisms ,which support to the reduction hypothesis.**

## (iii). The escape hypothesis

**The escape hypothesis considers viruses to have evolved from genetic material of the host cell that escaped from its control and developed autonomous evolving abilities . The support of this theory comes from the observation that modern day viruses can act as mediators of gene transfer and pick-pocket genes from their cellular hosts, a mechanism known a**

**horizontal gene transfer (HGT). Some scientists believe that HGT has been a dominant force in shaping the viral promote . This theory, however, fails to explain the presence of structures and genetic material in viruses that have no homology in the cellular world .**

## *Status of viruses in the living world*

**Viruses are generally regarded as neither living nor non-living . They are entirely dependent upon the host cells for reproduction and for this reason are considered to be obligate extracellular parasites . Viruses however follow both the biologically active and inactive life cycles. Once inside the cells, they either follow the 'lyric life cycle' during which they lyre the cell and release viral progeny or the 'cryogenics life cycle' during which they integrate their genome into the host DNA and remain dormant . One of the striking findings to come out of the sequencing of human genome project was the realization that endogenous retroviruses account for nearly 8% of the**

**human genome . These endogenous retroviruses resemble modern day retroviruses and are considered to be the remnants of ancient viral infections . Outside the host cells, viruses are metabolically inactive and survive long periods of time as crystals (chemical objects) . Based on these realizations and dual life cycles (both biological and chemical), viruses are regarded as intermediates between living and non-living forms and considered to be at the border of living and non-living organisms.**

## Viruses with large genomes

**One important realization is that not all viruses have minute genomes. In particular, a large group of dsDNA viruses that infect Eukarya have large genomes with hundreds of genes . This group is known as Nucleo-Cytoplasmic Large DNA Viruses (NCLDV) and is apparently a monophyletic group that includes five major families of viruses including Poxviridae, Asfarviridae, Phycodnaviridae, Ascoviridae/Iridoviridae and Mimiviridae .**

**Unlike other viruses that are strictly dependent on the host cells for replication, NCLDV are not exclusively dependent . They encode several key proteins involved in the processes of DNA replication, translation, and DNA repair . Additionally, all the families of NCLDV share a conserved set of 9 genes that are present in all the families and 22 genes present in at least 3 out of 4 families . Presence of this conserved core suggests that NCLDV originated from a common ancestor that had a complex gene repertoire .**

*Mithridates*

**The most exciting addition to the NCLDV was the introduction of Mithridates. The first member of Mimiviridae, Acanthameoba polyphaga mimivirus (APMV) was identified in 2003 by researchers in France . APMV (simply mimivirus) is one of the largest and most complex viruses known to date and for that reason, it was initially mistakenly identified as gram-positive bacterium until its viral nature was described in 2003 .**

## The concept of a Tree of Life (ToL)

**The unusual gnomic and physical features of giant viruses argue for the inclusion of viruses, at least the ones with large genomes, into the universal tree of life (ToL) together with the cellular protegees of Archaea, Bacteria and Eukarya. The ToL is a model that explains diversification of living organisms into three distinct superkingdoms i.e., Archaea, Bacteria and Eukarya. It was first described by Carl Woese who identified Archaea as a distinct domain of life and proposed the three-domain classification system . Prior to Woese's work, the organisms of the ToL were divided into prokaryotic and eukaryotic groups.**

**Discovery of giant viruses encouraged scientists to place viruses on the global evolutionary scale. Initial phylogenomic analysis based on the concatenation of seven**

**universally conserved proteins (Arg-tRNA synthetase, Met-tRNA synthetase, Tyr-tRNA synthetase, RNA polymerase II largest subunit, RNA polymerase II second largest subunit, Proliferating cell nuclear antigen, and 5'-3' exonuclease) in the proteomes of mimivirus, Archaea, Bacteria and Eukarya placed mimivirus at the base of Eukarya and identified mimivirus as a distinct superkingdom in the ToL . This study was challenged and future analysis involving individual proteins, rather than the concatenated set nested mimivirus consistently within Eukarya and close to amoeba (the cellular host of mimivirus) . Microbiologists proposed that previous analysis was flawed due to the use of concatenated protein sequences that could produce misleading trees if proteins evolved by different evolutionary mechanisms . Nesting of mimivirus within Eukarya suggested that the gene repertoire of mimivirus was acquired from amoeba by HGT . These experiments highlight the differences in the methods used to build phylogeny trees (e.g., concatenated set VS individual sequences) and suggest that HGT has tailored the proteome of mimiviruses. However, both these analyses used only a limited number of species and a very small set of proteins. Increased sampling of species from Archaea, Bacteria, Eukarya and a large number of giant viruses coupled with a phylogenetic model that is robust against the artifacts described above appears to be the most likely solution to study the origins of viruses and life itself. Identifying the right approach for ToL reconstruction is important**

**In general, there are two main approaches, sequence-based approaches that utilize nucleic acid or protein sequence information and structure-based approaches that focus on molecular structural information.**

# VIRAL CULTURE

**A viral culture is a test to find viruses that can cause an infection. A sample of body fluid or tissue is collected and added to certain cells used to grow a virus. If no virus infects the cells, the culture is negative. If a virus that can cause infection infects the cells, the culture is positive.**

## Method of culturing viruses

**Viruses can be grown in vivo (within a whole living organism, plant, or animal) or in vitro (outside a living organism in cells in an artificial environment, such as a test tube, cell culture flask, or agar plate).**

**There are three methods to cultivate viruses:**

**Cultivation of viruses can be discussed under following headings: Animal Inoculation. Inoculation into embryonated egg. Cell Culture.10-Aug-2022**

**There are 5 steps of a virus**

**The life cycle of virus. The virus life cycle could be divided into six steps: attachment, penetration, uncoating, gene expression and replication, assembly, and release.**

**(i) There are 7 characteristics of a virus. They are as follows:**

- **Non living structures.**
- **Non-cellular.**
- **Contain a protein coat called the capsid.**
- **Have a nucleic acid core containing DNA or RNA (one or the other - not both)**
- **Capable of reproducing only when inside a HOST cell.**

**. very very tiny infectious particle or it is a typical type of infectious particle • Size :- Ranges from 10 to 300 nm ( nano meter). Typical size is 100 nm. Virus is 100 times smaller than Erythrocyte cell.**

**Virus is very complex tiny particle, it is composed with different type of complex Nucleic acid (RNA and DNA). Capsized (Capsomers protein) :- Helical and Icosahedral symmetry Envelope Protiens (Glycopeoteins) Virus infects to the specific host cells based on suitable receptors. CHARACTERISTICS of VIRUSES**

**• It is a tiny complex infectious particle and it cannot be seen by ordinary microscope, normally it can be examined identified**

**The cell cultures are used for the isolation of viruses from clinical specimens for diagnosis of viral disease. It is also useful for biochemical studies of viral replication, and the production of viral antigens and vaccines. Depending upon the number of divisions that a cell line undergoes in vitro before dying. The cell lines have been classified as primary cell lines, diploid and continuous cell lines. Primary cell lines are often from fetal organs or tissues and have 5 or 10 divisions whereas diploid cell lines are a number of divisions in a culture that is roughly related to the life span of the species of animal. e.g. 50 for fetal human cells while 10 for fetal cells from horses and cows. Continuous cell lines are cells of a single type capable of indefinite propagation in vitro.**

**The most commonly used cell culture system in most laboratories includes chick embryo fibro blast cells, human amnion cells, Rhesus monkey kidney cells, HeLa (Human carcinoma of cervix cell line), Hep 2 (Human epithelium of larynx cell line), McCoy (Human synovial**

**carcinoma cell line), Vero (Vervet monkey kidney cell line), and W1-38 (Human embryonic lung cell line).**

**Principle of Virus Cultivation in the Cell lines**

**Viruses infect healthy cells that grow in the laboratory. When susceptible cells are used for the inoculation of viruses, they show pathological change,s and viruses, they show pathological changes, and viruses can be harvested from the cells for further tests. The growth of viruses in the cell line can be known by a) cytopathic effects, b) immunofluorescence, c) haemagglutination and haemadsorption, and haemadsorption, and d) interference.**

**Many viruses kill the infected viral cells in which they grow and bring about detectable changes in the morphology of the cells. These changes are collectively known as cytopathic effects. Some viruses however do not express any cytopathic effect (e.g., rubella virus)**

**The most important precaution to be taken during the maintenance of cell lines is sterility. Contamination of cell lines should be prevented and even cross-contamination among cell lines should be avoided.**

**Requirements for Virus Cultivation in the Cell lines**

**The following are the requirements for Virus Cultivation in the Cell lines –**

- **Inverted microscope**

- **Incubator**
- **Hemocytometer**
- **Biosafety cabinet (BSC)**
- **Sterile glassware**
- **Pre-sterilized tissue culture plasticware**
- **Pasteur pipettes and measuring pipettes**
- **Membrane filter**
- **Syringes**
- **Vials**
- **Discard jar**
- **Eagle's minimum essential medium (MEM)**
- **sodium bicarbonate (NaHCO3)**
- **EDTA trypsin mixture**
- **Fetal calf serum (FCS)**
- **Sterile double distilled water**
- **Virus inoculum,**
- **70% Ethanol/ spirit and sodium hypochlorite**
- **A monolayer of cell culture in a culture flask is treated with trypsin or versene to disperse cells.**
- **Specimen: Suspected virus-infected specimen like the cerebrospinal fluid (CSF), stool, rectal swab, throat swab, etc.**

## Procedure of Virus Cultivation in the Cell lines

1. **Discard the trypsin versene mixture and add a small amount of MEM with 10% FCS to the monolayer of cells.**

2. **Count the cells with the medium in a hectometer for appropriate splitting in the Cell lines.**
3. **The cell lines are observed for any cytological alterations that are diagnostic of viral infections. Inoculate the cells into sterile flasks or tubs for viral inoculation.**
4. **Fill the new flask with MEM and incubate in a horizontal position.**
5. **Select a healthy monolayer, which is also confluent, for viral inoculation.**
6. **Inoculate the monolayer of cells with the virus using a sterile Pasture pipette, and incubate at 37°C.**
7. **Observe for the cytopathic effect (CPE) 7 days after inoculation.**

## Quality Control

1. **Sterility precautions should be taken perfectly.**
2. **Susceptible cells are to be selected for the appropriate virus.**

## Observations

- **After incubation, the flasks are observed for confluency, and healthy monolayer cells; and virus-infected cells are classified.**
- **Viruses are known to produce cytopathic effects are identified by observing the same in the infected cell lines.**

- **Non- cytopathogenic viruses are identified by other methods like immunofluorescence, haemagglutination and haemadsorption, and interference.**

**The important observations for Virus Cultivation in the Cell lines are as follows:**

1. **The main purpose of virus cultivation is to isolate and identify viruses in clinical samples, to do research on the viral structure, replication, genetics, and effects on the host cells, and to prepare viruses for vaccine production.**
2. **The most important aspect to be taken care of in cell cultures is sterility. Hence precautions for sterility should be meticulously followed.**

   **Susceptible cells should be selected for appropriate viral inoculations.**

**We are very much grateful and and thankful for the in*clusion of some part here from the***

***COVID-19:***

**During the first year of the coronavirus pandemic, the virus didn't change that much. SARS-CoV-2 picked up only about one or two mutations each month.**

**Then in December 2020, the course of the pandemic shifted. Scientists in South Africa and the U.K. detected the first two variants of concern: alpha and beta. All of a sudden, the virus began to change rapidly. Instead of having only a few mutations as earlier variants did, these variants had around 20 mutations each.**

**The future of the pandemic is looking clearer as we learn more about infection**

**At the same time, the SARS-CoV-2 family tree grew more complex and interesting. Branches for a bunch of variants sprouted off the main trunk. Gamma, lambda and mu appeared (although none of these variants ended up spreading across the globe). And up at the top of the tree,**

**dozens of delta branches formed a broad overarching canopy.**

**We now understand how SARS-CoV-2 is evolving and how this family tree is going to grow. The future appeared clear again. The next variants of concern would emerge at the top of the tree, from the delta canopy. We should focus of genomics surveillance to identify sub-lineages of Delta variant. It's almost as if this massive branch on the SARS-CoV-2 family tree just appeared one day out of thin air, without any warning or signs that it was growing. And the initial highly transmissible omicron variant and its sibling BA.2 were at the end of the branch, ready to spread explosively around the world. Omicron BA.1 went on to sweep the world; BA.2 is now reported to be taking over in South Africa. (A third sibling also appeared, but so far it doesn't seem able to keep up with its globe-trotting siblings.) Another possibility is that this omicron branch did grow slowly over time, but for some unknown reason, scientists couldn't see it. It was in effect invisible. Perhaps because the virus was evolving inside another animal, like a rodent, and then jumped back into people. Perhaps because the virus was evolving very rapidly inside a person who had a chronic infection. Or perhaps because the virus**

**was spreading in parts of Africa that scientists weren't watching closely enough.**

***Genomic comparisons between Archaea, Bacteria, and Eukarya indicate that there are three main categories of organisms They are as follows:***

(i) ***In fact, a prevailing hypothesis derived from genomic and other comparisons say that the first eukaryote actually evolved from the interaction of an archaeon and a bacterium. Scientists study the structure and function of mitochondria and chloroplasts as well as their separate genomes to see what evidence might be left of the entities.***

**(ii) Scientists are likely unaware of a pool of SARS-CoV-2 variants that are replicating, mutating and evolving over time, completely under the radar. According to Hodcroft , there could be several other long — and invisible — branches growing on the SARS-CoV-2 tree, . And in the coming months, one of those branches could sprout off another family of rapidly spreading variants, similar to omicron. On the surface, this uncertainty about the coronavirus seems a bit scary. It raises the possibility that a new variant could crop up that's more lethal than any previous The "Omicron cluster is highly ... distinct from any known VOC [variant of concern] or variants of interest (VOI) and from any other lineages known to be**

**circulating in southern Africa," bioinformatician Tulio de Oliveira and his colleagues, who discovered the variant, wrote in the journal Nature in January 2021. It's almost as if this massive branch on the SARS-CoV-2 family tree just appeared one day out of thin air, without any warning or signs that it was growing. And the initial highly transmissible omicron variant and its sibling BA.2 were at the end of the branch, ready to spread explosively around the world. Omicron BA.1 went on to sweep the world; BA.2 is now reported to be taking over in South Africa. (A third sibling also appeared, but so far it doesn't seem able to keep up with its globe-trotting siblings.) Another possibility is that this omicron branch did grow slowly over time, but for some unknown reason, scientists couldn't see it. It was in effect invisible. Perhaps because the virus was evolving inside another animal, like a rodent, and then jumped back into people. P**

**(iii) erhaps because the virus was evolving very rapidly inside a person who had a chronic infection. Or perhaps beca**

**(iv) use the virus was spreading in parts of Africa that scientists weren't watching closely enough. Till now,one knows which hypothesis is correct. And this gap in our knowledge brings much uncertainty about the future of the pandemic. It means scientists are likely unaware of a pool of SARS-CoV-2 variants that are replicating, mutating and evolving over time, completely under the radar. According to virologist William Gallaher on the site**

**Virological.org. "The discomfort in discovering an entirely new and widely divergent VOC [variant of concern] ... is very real," writes Gallaher, who's at LSU Health New Orleans. "Beyond the medical impact of the Omicron variants, there is every reason to believe that this will happen yet again, as it did for Delta and now with Omicron." Right now, there could be several other long — and invisible — branches growing on the SARS-CoV-2 tree. And in the coming months, one of those branches could sprout off another family of rapidly spreading variants, similar to omicron. On the surface, this uncertainty about the coronavirus seems a bit scary. It raises the possibility that a new variant could crop up that's more lethal than any previous variant. Accoding to physician Roby Bhattacharyya, who's an infectious disease specialist at Massachusetts General Hospital and Harvard Medical School, U.S.A. "Variants that transmit better are going to be selected for, and it's kind of the luck of the draw whether that variant is also more severe or less severe. "Remarkably, however, our immune systems seem ready to handle whatever variant emerges. No matter what variant the coronavirus has thrown at us, including omicron, prior exposure to the virus (through either vaccination or a prior infection) has still offered good protection against hospitalization and severe disease.**

***ORIGIN OF COVID-19:***

**One of the biggest outstanding questions of the COVID-19 pandemic is the origin of SARS-CoV-2, the corona virus responsible for the disease. One idea, put forward by some news sites like Fox News and government officials , is that SARS-CoV-2 was man-made. As very few living people have witnessed a pandemic of this scale before, it is natural to wonder whether this could happen without human intervention. Furthermore, the presence of a research laboratory in Wuhan, China, the epicenter of the pandemic and known for its research on corona viruses, seemed a troubling coincidence. It is important for such a hypothesis to be considered, investigated, and evaluated along with other hypotheses about the origin of SARS-CoV-2.There are various arguments put forward to demonstrate that SARS-CoV-2 was man-made, such as the presence of genetic sequences from HIV or the presence of small artificial genetic sequences called pShuttles. However, according to virology research, the most likely origin of SARS-CoV-2 is zoonotic, meaning the virus jumped from an animal host to humans. The animal host for SARS-CoV-2 has not been identified yet.**

**However, a different form of the hypothesis that SARS-CoV-2 was man-made also circulated on social media and in various articles. This hypothesis involves the claim that**

**researchers used other corona viruses as templates to engineer SARS-CoV-2. Specifically, this hypothesis suggests that scientists modified a bat corona virus to produce SARS-CoV-2 based on the genetic similarities between SARS-CoV-2 and some bat corona viruses. For instance, a preprint published by virologist Li-Meng Yan claimed that two other bat corona viruses, ZC45 and ZXC21, provided the genetic backbone for scientists to artificially create SARS-CoV-2. In support of this claim, Yan pointed to the 100% identity shared in some parts of the genomes of SARS-CoV-2 and the bat corona viruses. Other virologists refuted this hypothesis and highlighted that the genetic sequences of ZC45 and ZXC21 are very different from that of SARS-CoV-2. This hypothesis was discussed again by Fox News in a segment aired on 28 February 2021. Steve Hilton noted that a bat corona virus, RaTG13, is currently the closest known virus to SARS-CoV-2 and shares 96.2% genetic identity with SARS-CoV-2. Fox News claimed that the 4% of genetic difference "is in the exact places where gain-of-function techniques would be used to make the virus more contagious. In technical language: the Spike receptor binding domain and furin cleavage site". The Spike receptor binding domain (RBD) is part of the Spike protein located on the surface of SARS-CoV-2, which enables the virus to latch onto its target cells and infect them. The molecular structure and composition of the Spike RBD is crucial because it dictates the infectivity of the virus. The emergence of several**

**SARS-CoV-2 variants in the course of the pandemic in the UK and South Africa is tied to specific changes in the Spike RBD. The furin cleavage site is a specific molecular structure within the RBD that improves the virus' ability to penetrate the target cells, making it more infectious. The so-called gain-of-function experiments that Fox News referred to are genetic techniques used in microbiology to alter specific functions in viral or bacterial strains that were not present in the original strain, such as increasing yields or reducing replication abilities. According to the U.S. Department of Health and Human Services, a gain-of-function study "improves the ability of a pathogen to cause disease". In essence, Fox News suggested that researchers replaced the original Spike RBD from RaTG13 with a new, man-made RBD equipped with a furin cleavage site, resulting in that 4% genetic difference and giving birth to the highly-infectious SARS-CoV-2. However, this hypothesis is scientifically unsound for several reasons . Specifically, we explain why the hypothesis that other corona viruses served as a template for engineering a new virus is unlikely and how it conflicts with what we know about these viruses and the current state of genetic engineering technology. The bat coronavirus RaTG13 couldn't be a template for SARS-CoV-2; the genetic gap between the two is too wide to be bridged by engineering. Health Feedback reached out to several experts in virology, who unanimously rejected the hypothesis that the**

**bat coronavirus RaTG13 served as a template to engineer SARS-CoV-2.**

**Firstly, David Robertson, a professor of viral genomics at the University of Glasgow, explained that it is inaccurate to claim that the 4% of genetic difference between the two viruses are entirely confined to the Spike RBD. "The replacement of RaTG13 RBD with SARS-CoV-2 RBD would still be a relatively divergent virus from SARS-CoV-2. This is because there are other mutations in RaTG13's genome that make it distinct from SARS-CoV-2," he said. In other words, there are genetic differences in several parts of the genome. Therefore, simply swapping out the original RBD of RaTG13 for a new man-made RBD would not produce the genomic sequence of SARS-CoV-2, since differences in the virus' genetic code would still remain in other parts of its genome.**

**Robert Garry, a professor of microbiology at the University of Tulane, concurred: "While 96% sounds close, in evolutionary terms, it is quite distant, and it would take decades of evolution for the genome of RaTG13 to resemble that of SARS-CoV-2. The difference is about 1,200 bases or 400 amino acids. Gain-of-function research cannot close that gap." He added, "This would require a virus much closer than RaTG13, at least 99% similar or more likely 99.9% similar".The reviewers also highlighted another limitation of this hypothesis. In order for scientists to genetically engineer SARS-CoV-2 from RaTG13, they**

**must have known which Spike RBD to use to replace RaTG13's original one. However, researchers didn't discover a Spike RBD similar to the one of SARS-CoV-2 before the pandemic. Given this knowledge gap, there is no plausible scenario to explain how scientists engineered the exact genetic sequence seen in the SARS-CoV-2 Spike protein RBD, since it was unknown to scientists until after the outbreak.**

**As Stanley Perlman, a professor of microbiology at the University of Iowa, said, "it would not be known in advance what sequence should be used to replace the RaTG13 Spike protein." Susan Weiss, a professor of microbiology at the University of Pennsylvania countered the hypothesis with the question: "Where would they get the RBD from to insert into RaTG13?"**

**After the SARS outbreak in 2003, which was caused by another corona virus, SARS-CoV-1, researchers identified a set of key amino acids within the Spike RBD important for SARS-CoV-1 infectiousness. To improve the infectiousness of a corona virus, the best engineering strategy would have been to use the amino acid sequences discovered in SARS-CoV-1, as these are known to be efficient and can then be refined to produce an even better molecular design for SARS-CoV-2.**

**Surprisingly, the current SARS-CoV-2 Spike RBD doesn't contain this optimal set of amino acids recognized in SARS-CoV-1, yet it is nonetheless able to bind to its target**

**human cells with an affinity even higher than SARS-CoV-1. This finding ( Ref *) undermines the claim that SARS-CoV-2 is the result of modifying RaTG13 to give it an enhanced Spike RBD.**

**There is neither evidence nor a plausible scenario for scientists to engineer SARS-CoV-2 through gain-of-function experiments.**

**The scientists who evaluated this claim also considered a hypothetical scenario in which scientists produced SARS-CoV-2 through gain-of-function experiments, but using a template other than RaTG13. They unanimously deemed it very unlikely that SARS-CoV-2 originated from such gain-of-function experiments.**

**Commenting on this, Kristian Andersen, a professor of immunology at Scripps Research, said that "there is no way gain-of-function could have created SARS-CoV-2 from RaTG13".**

**Robertson stated that "It's extremely unlikely SARS-CoV-2 was generated by gain-of-function experiments [Ref. *] Moreover all of the properties of SARS-CoV-2 can be explained by natural processes, such as a mutation and recombination that are well-documented in corona viruses".**

**Furthermore, researchers highlighted that corona virus manipulation is so difficult that it is extremely unlikely that scientists engineered SARS-CoV-2 through gain-of-**

**function experiments. Weiss said that "it is not easy to design viruses to behave the way you might predict—I believe that SARS-CoV-2 was selected in nature and not designed". Likewise, Perlman stated, "Finally the whole process of reverse genetics for corona viruses is difficult, even for experts. So my answer is that it is very unlikely (impossible) for this scenario to be the explanation."**

**In summary, the weight of the scientific evidence indicates that the bat coronavirus RaTG13 couldn't have served as a backbone for engineering SARS-CoV-2. Despite some similarities, there are too many genetic differences scattered across their genomes for RaTG13 to serve as a template for SARS-CoV-2. (Ref,*)**

**In addition, even if one decided to create a corona virus capable of causing a pandemic, there is no plausible scientific rationale justifying the choice of RaTG13 as a backbone or the design of the SARS-CoV-2 Spike RBD. Scientific experts in virology found it very unlikely that gain-of-function experiments could create a virus similar to SARS-CoV-2. The simplest explanation—the hypothesis that requires the least "ifs" and "maybes"—is that SARS-CoV-2 is the product of natural selection in the wild and was transmitted from animals to humans in a process that has occurred repeatedly throughout history.**

**Fox News is confusing "Gain of Function Research" and "Basic Research". The bat research performed at the Wuhan Institute of Virology [of which] EcoHealth was a part, was basic research – and in fact, was instrumental in our ability to respond quickly when SARS-CoV-2 emerged. There's absolutely no validity to the claim [that gain-of-function] experiments could have created SARS-CoV-2 – there is no way gain-of -function could have created SARS-CoV-2 from RaTG13.**

**David Robertson, Professor, University of Glasgow explained the following observations:**

- **Is it likely that SARS-CoV-2 is derived from RaTG13 by artificially replacing the Spike RBD?**

**Virologists say that the replacement of RaTG13's RBD with SARS-CoV-2's RBD would still be a relatively divergent virus from SARS-CoV-2. This is because there are other mutations in RaTG13's genome that make it distinct from SARS-CoV-2. Virologists have to change these other parts of RaTG13's genome to arrive at SARS-CoV-2's sequence. (Ref.*)**

- **Is it likely that SARS-CoV-2 is the result of gain-of-function experiments?**

**It's extremely unlikely SARS-CoV-2 was generated by gain-of-function experiments. We didn't know anything**

**about this new corona virus before it emerged in 2019 so how could it have been designed? What would have been the template for this? It's just incredibly implausible that some random experiments could have generated a virus with such dramatic properties but so unlike anything we'd observed before.**

**Moreover all of the properties of SARS-CoV-2 can be explained by natural processes such as a mutation and recombination that are well documented in corona viruses. We discussed the probable source of the SARS-CoV-2 progenitor here in a study by virologists.**

**Susan Weiss, Professor, University of Pennsylvania writes:**

- **Is it likely that SARS-CoV-2 is derived from RaTG13 by artificially replacing the Spike RBD?**

**Virologists say the RBD is not the only difference between the two genomes. They would have to make many other changes. Where would they get the RBD from to insert into RaTG13? Why would they suppose that changing the RBD of some random bat virus would produce a virus lethal for humans? These viruses are naturally selected to do what they do—just as variants now are selected to optimize stability and spread.**

- **Is it likely that SARS-CoV-2 is the result of gain-of-function experiments?**

**Virologists do not think so for similar reasons as above. No diabolic genius could figure out how to design a virus to behave this way. Where would you start—why RaTG13? It makes no sense .**

**Virologists remembered two types of engineering Virologists attempted many years ago with murine coronavirus. In one set of experiments, they constructed viruses with chimeric spike proteins (S1 and S2 from closely related strains and some other combinations). These viruses replicated well in cell culture, but were quite dead in animals. The point being: Virologists tried to engineer corona viruses from closely related strains and it did not give us pathogenic viruses. ( Ref.*)**

**In another case, virologists exchanged a furin site for a sequence from a closely related strain that did not have a furin site. The new virus replicated well in cultures, but did not cause disease in mice. On the other hand, when they let the virus be selected for persistence in mouse glial cells, they obtained variants with a mutant cleavage site—which arose through natural selection —and they were quite pathogenic in the brain but had lost liver tropism [meaning that the virus could not infect cells from the liver anymore]. Main point is not easy to design viruses to behave the way they might predict and believe that SARS-CoV-2 was selected in nature and not designed.**

**Robert Garry, Professor, University of Tulane says:**

**RatG13 could not have served as the backbone of SARS-CoV-2. While 96% sounds close, in evolutionary terms, it is quite distant, and it would take decades of evolution for the genome of RaTG13 to resemble that of SARS-CoV-2. The difference is about 1,200 bases or 400 amino acids. Gain-of-function research cannot close that gap. Passage in cell culture or transgenic animals would never create the changes. Replacing the RaTG13 RBD with the RBD of another virus (such as the pangolin corona virus) certainly would not close the gap. It still leaves you with a virus that is still 96% different from SARS-CoV-2. It is highly unlikely, in fact,near impossible—that SARS-CoV-2 is the result of gain-of-function research. This would require a virus much closer than RaTG13, at least 99% similar or more likely 99.9% similar.**

**Stanley Perlman, Professor, University of Iowa says:**

- **Is it likely that SARS-CoV-2 is derived from RaTG13 by artificially replacing the Spike RBD?**

**RaTG13 is 4% different from SARS-CoV-2. This is equivalent to 1,200 nucleotide. Virologists do not know what fraction of the differences between SARS-CoV-2 and RaTG13 are in the S protein; there are certainly some outside of the [Spike RBD] protein. (REF. *)**

**In addition, it would not be known in advance what sequence should be used to replace the RaTG13 S protein. Finally, the whole process of reverse genetics for corona viruses is difficult, even for experts. So the answer is that it is very unlikely (impossible) for this scenario to be the explanation. It is much more likely that nature did this.**

- **Is it likely that SARS-CoV-2 is the result of gain-of-function experiments?**

**This possibility implies that a virus was already in hand that was known to infect human cells. There is no evidence for this. Even if this putative virus existed, it would not be known in advance how to modify it to enhance transmission and virulence. Passage through tissue culture cells generally results in virus attenuation. In fact, that is how the poliovirus vaccine was developed from wild type polio.**

**Christian Stevens from the Benhur Lee lab at the Mount Sinai School of Medicine has provided a comprehensive explanation of the multiple scientific studies examining the origin of the coronavirus.**

**RaTG13 is the closest related coronavirus genome phylogenetically to SARS-CoV-2, consequently understanding its provenance is of key importance to understanding the**

**origin of the COVID-19 pandemic. The RaTG13 NGS dataset is attributed to a fecal swab from the intermediate horseshoe bat Rhinolophus affinis. However, sequence analysis reveals that this is unlikely. Metagenomic analysis using Metaxa2 shows that only 10.3 % of small subunit (SSU) rRNA sequences in the dataset are bacterial, inconsistent with a fecal sample, which are typically dominated by bacterial sequences.(REF.*)**

**In addition, the bacterial taxa present in the sample are inconsistent with fecal material.**

**Assembly of mitochondrial SSU rRNA sequences in the dataset produces a contiguity of 98.7 % identical to R.affinis mitochondrial SSU rRNA, indicating that the sample was generated from this or a closely related species. 87.5 % of the NGS reads map to the Rhinolophus ferrumequinum genome, the closest bat genome to R.affinis available. In the annotated genome assembly, 62.2 % of mapped reads map to protein coding genes. These results clearly demonstrate that the dataset represents a Rhinolophus sp, transcription, and not a fecal swab sample. Overall, the data show that the RaTG13 data set was generated by the Wuhan Institute of Virology (WIV) from a transcriptome derived from Rhinolophus sp. tissue or cell line, indicating that RaTG13 was in live culture. This raises the question of whether the WIV was culturing additional unreported**

**coronaviruses closely related to SARS-CoV-2 prior to the pandemic. The implications for the origin of the COVID-19 pandemic are discussed. Understanding the origin of severe acute respiratory syndrome coronavirus 2 (SARSCoV-2) and coronavirus disease 2019 (COVID-19) is vital for preventing future pandemics. There are two main hypotheses regarding the origin of the COVID-19 pandemic. The zoonosis hypothesis proposes that the progenitor of SARS-CoV-2 jumped from a bat or intermediate host to a human . This scenario requires that the**

**infected bat or intermediate host came into close contact with a human in a non research(REF.*) setting which allowed the transmission to occur. The contrasting lab leak hypothesis proposes that SARS-CoV-2 was transmitted into the human population from a research related activity such as a laboratory experiment .**

**The RaTG13 coronavirus genome, sequenced by the Wuhan Institute of Virology (WIV), is phylogenetically the closest known relative to SARS-CoV-21, and its apparent provenance from the intermediate horseshoe bat Rhinolophus affinis has been used to support the proposed zoonotic origin of SARS-CoV-2 . However, the original Nature publication describing the RaTG13 genome sequence was sparse regarding sampling location and date of sequencing of RaTG13. A fragment of the RNA dependent RNA polymerase (RdRp) was the first part of RaTG13 to be sequenced, initially labelled as**

**'RaBtCov/4991' , and subsequently renamed 'RaTG13' in the Nature paper (the link between the two was identified . Further details were elaborated in an Addendum, which gave the date of sequencing of RaTG13 as 2018, and the sampling location as a mine in Mojiang, Yunnan Province, China, which had been associated with the death in 2012 of three miners who had been clearing bat guano, from a virus like respiratory infection . While RaTG13 shows 96.2 % sequence identity with the SARS-CoV-2 genome , a new Rhinolophus malayanus sarbecovirus genome from Laos, BANAL-52 , shows 96.9 % nucleotide sequence identity with SARS-CoV-2 (data not shown). However, a maximum likelihood phylogenomic tree shows that RaTG13 is the closest relative to SARS-CoV-2, with strong support. Clearly, the provenance of RaTG13 is of great importance in determining the origin of the COVID-19 outbreak, whether by zoonosis, or by a lab leak event. However, a number of preprints and publications have identified potential problems with the RaTG13 raw sequence data. In particular, database entries for the raw reads deposited on the GSA, Short Read Archive (SRA) and European Nucleotide Archive (ENA) state that the data were generated from a R.affinis fecal swab. In addition, the original paper describing the detection of RaTG13 RdRp (then**

**labelled 'RaBtCov/4991'), stated that the sequence was obtained from a fecal swab . Likewise, a Master's thesis from the WIV describing the sequencing of the RaTG13 genome (labelled in the thesis as 'Ra4991_Yunnan'), attributed the provenance of the sample to one of 2815 anal swabs/fecal pellets collected from Yunnan Province, China**
**from 2011-2016 . However, a low proportion of bacteria-related reads is indicated by a taxonomic analysis of the raw reads on the dataset's SRA webpage, and appears inconsistent with a fecal swab .**

***We are very much thankful and grateful for the the inclusion of some portion here from the article of the Research article : Open Access Published: 21 January 202 PREFACE1; Horizontal gene transfer and recombination analysis of SARS-CoV-2 genes helps discover its close relatives and shed light on its origin***

- ***Vladimir Makarenkov, Bogdan Mazoure,***
- ***Guillaume Rabusseau & Pierre Legendre***

***BMC Ecology and Evolution volume 21, Article number: 5 (2021) Cite this article***

***https://doi.org/10.1186/s12862-***

***ROLE OF COVID-19 IN HEART ATTACK***

# Cardiologists explain what we now know about the connection between heart disease and COVID-19. COVID-19 injures the heart and it causes cardiac manifestations.

**(i) In Covid-19 patients, cardiac enzymes test is essential. These tests measure the enzymes and proteins that increase when our heart is damaged, including troponin and creatine kinase (CK). Damage to heart muscle cells causes troponin and creatine kinase to leak out of the heart into the blood. High levels of these enzymes on blood tests are a clear sign the heart's in trouble. "The presence of these enzymes identifies heart attacks.**

**(ii) COVID-19 causes myocarditis, which can lead to heart failure and arrhythmias**

**(iii) Coronavirus can also cause dangerous inflammation in the heart, or myocarditis, which prevents the heart from doing its job effectively. COVID-19 infection can directly damage the heart and cause arrhythmias and heart failure.**

**(iv)For COVID-19 patients who are experiencing heart failure, doctors measure brain natriuretic peptide (BNP) levels. "When the heart muscle stretches, this protein gets released into the bloodstream.If BNP levels are elevated in COVID-19 patients, that means there's heart injury and heart failure, which translates into potentially higher risks for worse outcomes, causing death.**

**(iv) COVID-19 infection increases blood clots and has been observed that it can cause a dramatic increase in blood clots throughout the body. Blood clots happen when our blood forms gel-like clumps. We know from other infectious processes, such as sepsis or bacterial or viral illnesses, that people can have disruption of their clotting system. They either have bleeding problems or clotting problems. There's some suspicion that the coronavirus has a direct effect on the clotting system as well. That may be why we're seeing not only stroke, but clots in small blood vessels and microclots in the lungs and heart."**

**But in the ultimate catch-22, having a healthy immune system can sometimes backfire. It can overreact to the virus and cause inflammation that affects the organs — a response known as a cytokine storm. "We don't know what makes someone more hyper inflammatory than someone else. Decent control of our immune system might leave us with a low-grade fever and cough. But an immune system in overdrive seems to drive cellular effects that infiltrate the heart and take us over the edge, causing heart muscle inflammation and weakness."**

**The COVID-19 virus enters cells via a receptor called ACE2, or angiotensin converting enzyme-2. It is established fact that if we take an ACE inhibitor or ARB, it might increase the activity of this ACE2, and in theory, increase the entry of the virus into the cell."**

**Although COVID-19 — the disease caused by the coronavirus that's led to the global pandemic — is primarily a respiratory or lung disease, the heart can also suffer.**

**Research scientists explain that cells in the lung and heart are both covered with protein molecules called angiotensin-converting enzyme 2, or ACE-2. The ACE-2 protein is the doorway that the new coronavirus uses to enter cells and multiply. ACE-2 normally plays a favorable role in protecting tissue by being anti-inflammatory. But if the new coronavirus somehow disables those molecules, these cells may be left unprotected when the immune system springs into action.**

**"There are multiple mechanisms for heart damage in COVID-19, and not everyone is the same. Temporary or lasting damage to heart tissue can be due to several factors factors:**

**(i) Lack of oxygen. As the virus causes inflammation and fluid to fill up the air sacs in the lungs, less oxygen can reach the bloodstream. The heart has to work harder to pump blood through the body, which can be dangerous in people with pre-existing heart disease. The heart can fail from overwork, or insufficient oxygen can cause cell death and tissue damage in the heart and other organs.**

**(ii) Myocarditis: inflammation of the heart. The coronavirus may infect and damage the heart's muscle tissue directly, as is possible with other viral infections, including some strains of the flu. The heart may also**

**become damaged and inflamed indirectly by the body's own immune system response.**

**(iii) Stress cardiomyopathy. Viral infections can cause cardiomyopathy, a heart muscle disorder that affects the heart's ability to pump blood effectively. When attacked by a virus, the body undergoes stress and releases a surge of chemicals called catecholamines that can stun the heart. "Once the infection resolves, the stressor has ended and the heart can recover.**

*.We are very much thankful and obliged for the inclusion of some part of the article here from StatPearls [Internet].Cardiac Manifestations Of Coronavirus (COVID-19) Indranill Basu-Ray; Nureddin k.Almaddah;*

*AdedayoAdeboye; Michael P. Soos.*Author Information and Affiliations Last Update: May 2, 2022

*ACE2 Receptor*

**SARS-CoV-2 uses its S-spike to bind to ACE2 receptors as the point of entry. SARS-CoV-2 uses its S-spike to bind to ACE2 receptors as the point type 1 and type 2 pneumocytes and other cell types, including endothelial cells. ACE2 is an inverse regulator of the renin-angiotensin-aldosterone system. Like other coronaviruses,**

**SARS-CoV-2 uses these ACE2 receptors to target the respiratory system primarily.**

### *SARS-CoV-2 and the Immune Response*

**There are two immune-response phases of COVID-19 disease. Phase 1 occurs during the incubation stage of the disease, during which the adaptive immune system works to eliminate the virus; if any defects occur at this stage, SARS-CoV-2 will disseminate and induce systemic organ damage, with more significant destruction of organs with higher expression of ACE2 receptors, including lung, endothelial cells, the heart, and the kidneys. This massive damage leads to phase 2: severe inflammation in the affected organs.**

### *Mechanisms of Cardiac Damage in COVID-19*

**Multiple mechanisms have been suggested for cardiac damage, based on studies conducted during the previous SARS and MERS epidemics and the ongoing COVID-19 epidemic. Part of the systemic inflammatory response in severe COVID-19 is the release of high levels of cytokines (known as cytokine release syndrome) that can injure multiple tissues, including vascular endothelium and cardiac myocytes.**

### Cytokine Release Syndrome

**Cytokine release syndrome occurs in patients with severe COVID-19 infection. Many proinflammatory cytokines are**

**significantly elevated in severe cases, including interleukin (IL)-2, IL-10, IL-6, IL-8, and tumor necrosis factor (TNF)-α. Cytokines play an important role during infection with the virus (phase 1) and during ongoing severe inflammation (phase 2), resulting in acute respiratory distress syndrome (ARDS) and other end-organ damage.**

## Direct Myocardial Cell Injury

**The interaction of SARS-CoV-2 with ACE2 can cause changes to the ACE2 pathways, leading to acute injury of the lung, heart, and endothelial cells. A small number of case reports have indicated that SARS-CoV2 might directly infect the myocardium, causing viral myocarditis. However, in most cases, myocardial damage appeared to be caused by increased cardiometabolic demand associated with the systemic infection and ongoing hypoxia caused by severe pneumonia or ARDS.**

## Acute Coronary Syndrome

**Plaque rupture leading to acute coronary syndrome can result from the systemic inflammation and catecholamine surge inherent in this disease. Coronary thrombosis also has been identified as a possible cause of acute coronary syndrome in COVID-19 patients.**

## Other Possible Mechanisms

**Certain medications such as corticosteroids, antiviral medications, and immunological agents may have cardiotoxic side effects. Electrolyte disturbances can occur**

**in any critical systemic illness and trigger arrhythmias, for which patients with underlying cardiac disease are at higher risk. There is particular concern about hypokalemia in patients with COVID-19, given the interaction of SARS-CoV-2 with the renin-angiotensin-aldosterone system. Hypokalemia is well known to increase vulnerability to various kinds of arrhythmia.**

**COVID-19 disease mostly affects middle-aged and elderly patients. Children seem to be asymptomatic or get a mild form of the disease. The mean incubation period is about 5 days from exposure but ranges between 2 to 14 days. A higher risk of infection has been noticed in older patients, male sex, patients with medical comorbidities, patients with chronic pulmonary or chronic cardiac or chronic kidney disease, and patients with diabetes.U.S experience indicates that up to one-fifth of infected people are between the ages of 20 to 44 years who have been hospitalized, including 2% to 4% who required intensive care unit admission. The symptoms of COVID-19 are akin to other viral upper respiratory illnesses. Initial presentation can, however, be vague. GI symptoms are present in 10% of cases, including nausea, vomiting, or diarrhea. Patients may also experience rarely headaches and confusion. Atypical presentations of infection may be more common in the elderly and immunocompromised, who may not mount a febrile response. Alteration of taste and smell, anosmia, is suspected as an early symptom of**

**COVID-19 and is occasionally reported as a phenomenon of upper respiratory viral infection. Three major trajectories for COVID-19 have been described: a mild disease with upper respiratory symptoms, non-severe pneumonia, and severe pneumonia complicated by acute respiratory distress syndrome (ARDS), necessitating aggressive resuscitative measures. Based on current reports, which could be biased by available data, only hospitalized patients were noted to have cardiac involvement. Though, as alluded to earlier, this number is significant and did correlate with increased morbidity and mortality several notches higher than those without ARDS.**

**Certain laboratory anomalies have corresponded to cardiovascular involvement and severe illness. These include lymphopenia, elevated lactate dehydrogenase, liver enzymes, ferritin and C-reactive protein, prothrombin time, troponin, creatine phosphokinase, serum creatinine, and D-dimer.**

**Cardiac care needs to be optimized for COVID-19 patients with an aim for early detection and management of cardiac ailments with the simultaneous aim at triaging cases and proper protection to prevent or minimize COVID-19 exposure. As Bonow et al. have rightly put, the message to the patients should be clear that prompt emergency care to be sought in case of warning cardiac symptoms. Mask-wearing, physical distancing remains as**

**essential as ever. Simultaneously, doctors and researchers are finding the best practices for COVID-19 related cardiovascular disease.**

### *ACE inhibitors (ACEI)/ Angiotensin Receptor Blockers (ARB)*

### *Convalescent Plasma*

**Convalescent plasma for the treatment of COVID-19 patients is obtained from individuals who have recovered from COVID-19 and have generated an immune response. Small randomized trials and case studies have shown some benefit from convalescent plasma in hospitalized patients with severe COVID-19, especially if given early in the disease course. The FDA has granted emergency use authorization for convalescent plasma in hospitalized patients with COVID-19.**

### *Ivermectin*

**Ivermectin was introduced as a potential treatment for COVID-19 patients. Ivermectin is an antiparasitic drug used to treat Strongyloides and onchocerciasis infection. A Meta-analysis by Dr. Andrew Hill investigated Ivermectin in 18 randomized clinical trials. There was a 75% reduction in mortality found in moderate or severe infection in six randomized trials. In another randomized trial of 476 patients, Ivermectin did not shorten the duration of the infection. Multiorgan failure was reported**

**in four patients. The FDA has issued a warning against using Ivermectin to prevent or treat COVID-19 infection.**

**Vaccination**

**The SARS-CoV-2 genetic sequence was published in January 2020, and since then, researcher teams worldwide have been working actively to develop a vaccine against SARS-CoV-2. More than 90 vaccines are being developed at this time. The mRNA- based vaccines developed by Pfizer and Moderna have been granted emergency use authorization (EUA) by the US Food and Drug Administration (FDA). Many healthcare workers have already received these vaccines.**

**Immune thrombotic thrombocytopenia developed after ChAdOx1nCov-19 Vaccination was reported as a rare complication developed in several cases. Mechanism of the thrombocytopenia similar to heparin-induced thrombocytopenia.**

**No significant cardiac complication has been reported with any of the vaccines thus far.**

***Heart Failure***

**Heart failure has been well described in patients with pneumonia, and now multiple studies have shown an association between heart failure and COVID-19. In a case series of 21 severely ill patients with COVID-19 in an ICU, one-third developed new-onset cardiomyopathy with globally decreased left ventricular ejection fraction on**

**transthoracic echocardiogram with clinical signs of cardiogenic shock and elevated creatine kinase or troponin I. In a cohort of 191 patients with COVID-19 from Wuhan, 23% were diagnosed with heart failure; of the 54 patients who died, 52% had heart failure In another study of 799 COVID-19 patients from Wuhan, heart failure was observed in 24% of patients and 49% of those who died. Patients with COVID-19 may develop right-sided heart failure secondary to pulmonary hypertension due to hypoxia and ARDS. In a cohort of 105 COVID-19 patients hospitalized at one center, right ventricular dilation was present in 31% of intubated patients. Right ventricular hypokinesia was observed in 66% of COVID-19 patients with right ventricular enlargement versus 5% of COVID-19 patients without right ventricular enlargement. A few studies have reported takotsubo (stress-induced) cardiomyopathy as a complication of COVID-19. Most cases occurred in women older than 65 years of age. The association with COVID-19 infection is not clear, but it has been suggested that the emotional distress and anxiety associated with the pandemic may have a role in the onset of this disease.**

**The etiology of heart failure in COVID-19 disease is unclear whether it is a direct effect of SARS-CoV-2 on the myocardium or indirectly caused by hypoxia, cytokine release, volume overload, renal failure, stress, or overwhelming critical illness. Further, some patients with**

**risk factors for heart disease (diabetes, hypertension, hyperlipidemia, coronary artery disease) may have had underlying subclinical heart failure uncovered or exacerbated by COVID-19 infection and associated illness. Acute coronary syndromes triggered by COVID-19 can also result in heart failure or worsen the preexisting disease.**

**Diagnostic workup for suspected heart failure includes brain natriuretic peptide, troponin markers, transthoracic echocardiography, and cardiac MRI. Cardiac MRI may help look for changes induced by COVID-19 in patients with diastolic heart failure.**

**Knowledge of the presence or absence and degree of cardiomyopathy is crucial for managing patients in shock status and determining the need for circulatory support and type of extracorporeal membranous oxygenation. The management of heart failure in patients with COVID-19 should be initiated and continued as per current guidelines.**

## *Arrhythmias and Sudden Cardiac Arrest*

**Arrhythmias and sudden cardiac arrest have been reported with COVID-19. In a report of 138 hospitalized patients with COVID-19 in Wuhan, 17% had arrhythmias , although the specific types of arrhythmias were not described. In another study of hospitalized COVID-19 patients in Wuhan, 6% had developed ventricular tachycardia or ventricular fibrillation. More patients with elevated troponin T levels (17%) than normal troponin T levels (2%) had ventricular tachycardia or ventricular fibrillation**

**In patients with COVID-19, a cardiac injury that induces arrhythmia can be due to various causes, such as hypoxia, a worsening of coronary perfusion, direct tissue damage, hyperacute systemic inflammatory response syndrome, or the effects of medications used to manage the COVID-19. Hypokalemia can occur in patients with COVID-19 due to the interaction of SARS-CoV-2 with the renin-angiotensin-aldosterone system and increases vulnerability to various kinds of arrhythmia.Recommendations for managing arrhythmias are similar to those for non-COVID patients, including electrolyte optimization, avoidance of triggers, and medication modification. Concomitant ECG monitoring for patients who have long QTc or taking**

**medications known to prolong the QTc interval is mandated.**

**Cardiac arrest was reported in 11% of COVID-19 patients with ECG evidence of ST elevation in a case series from New York. A study from Italy looked at local out-of-hospital cardiac arrests during the first 40 days of the COVID-19 outbreak and compared the rate with that from the same period a year ago. During the study period, there was a 58% increase in out-of-the hospital cardiac arrests (362 cases compared to 229 cases the year before) correlating to the incidence of COVID-19. Of the 362 cases of out-of-hospital cardiac arrest, 28% had, or were suspected of having, COVID-19.**

*Thromboembolism and Coagulation Abnormalities*

**COVID-19 infection has been associated with venous and arterial thromboembolism. Studies have shown abnormalities of the coagulation cascade, with elevated D-dimer, thrombocytopenia, slightly elevated prothrombin time, and higher levels of fibrinogen and von Willebrand factor. The hypercoagulable state in COVID-19 infection is thought to be related to severe inflammatory response, cytokine storm, and endothelial damage, along with underlying patient comorbidities.**

**In a retrospective cohort study from China, a D-dimer >1 mcg/mL was reported in 42% of patients and in 81% of those who died from COVID-19; as such, it was identified**

**as one of the risk factors for death and was associated with 18-times increased risk for mortality. A Wuhan study found elevated D-dimer in 46% of patients, 60% of patients with severe illness, and up to 70% of patients in a composite group with ICU admission, mechanical ventilation, or death. Platelet count was <150,000/mm3 (signifying thrombocytopenia) in 36% of patients and 58% of patients with severe disease. In an autopsy series of COVID-19 patients from Germany, deep venous thrombosis was found in 58% of patients in whom venous thromboembolism was not suspected before death. Pulmonary embolism was found in 4 of the patients and was the direct cause of death**

**COVID-19 infection has been associated with cerebrovascular accidents. The incidence of acute ischemic stroke in patients with COVID-19 is approximately 1%–3%. A review of 37 studies with 370 patients with COVID-19 who had developed acute ischemic stroke or transient ischemic attack found that most patients had underlying comorbidities predisposing them to ischemic stroke. However, case reports describe large-vessel strokes in young adults with COVID-19 who did not have any cardiovascular risk factors. In a case series from the United Arab Emirates, 22 patients with confirmed COVID-19 infection presented with ischemic stroke symptoms as the first evidence of their COVID-19 infection; most were male and younger than 55 years of**

**age. Patients with COVID-19 and stroke are reported to have significantly higher mortality than historical controls. In addition to arterial strokes, cerebral venous sinus thrombosis has been reported in 13 patients in 9 studies.**

**Peripheral arterial thromboembolism causing acute limb ischemia also has been described in COVID-19. Two young patients without any known risk factors have been diagnosed with acute thrombosis involving the aorta presenting as acute limb ischemia. A report from Italy described four patients with COVID-19 who developed acute limb ischemia; two had comorbidities, but the other two were young and active, without any comorbidities. In another Italian case series, 20 patients were diagnosed with COVID-19-related pneumonia before acute limb ischemia was detected; revascularization was less successful than expected, possibly secondary to a virus-related hypercoagulable state. A case series from Spain described acute limb ischemia in four patients infected with COVID-19 secondary to a hypercoagulable state. None of these patients had known cardiovascular disease or comorbidities that could have predisposed them to arterial embolisms.**

**There is increasing evidence that anticoagulation is of benefit in COVID-19 illness. A study from New York demonstrated that treatment-dose anticoagulation was associated with reduced mortality. In the study, 786 out of**

**2773 patients (28%) were administered systemic anticoagulation. In-hospital mortality for patients who received anticoagulation was 23%, and median survival was 21 days, compared with 23% and median survival of 14 days in patients who did not receive treatment-dose anticoagulation. In patients who needed mechanical ventilation, in-hospital mortality was 29% for those who received treatment-dose anticoagulation, and median survival was 21 days, versus 63% and median survival of 9 days in patients who did not receive treatment-dose anticoagulation. A retrospective study from China showed that the use of low molecular weight heparin was associated with better prognosis in severe COVID-19 patients meeting sepsis-induced coagulopathy criteria or with markedly elevated D-dimer.**

**At this time, most centers have incorporated anticoagulation into the treatment protocol for COVID-19 patients, especially if they have elevated D-dimer levels. However, it is unknown which anticoagulation agent (unfractionated heparin, low-molecular-weight heparin, warfarin, or direct oral anticoagulants) is most efficacious in preventing thromboembolic events in COVID-19 patients. As always, the risks and benefits of anticoagulation treatment must be weighed for each patient. Future clinical trials may shed more light on the benefits of anticoagulation in COVID-19 infection.**

### *Acute Coronary Syndrome*

**Several studies and case reports have established an association between COVID-19 and acute coronary syndrome. In a letter to the editor, investigators from New York reported their experience with COVID-19 patients who showed ST-segment elevation on ECG. Ten patients had ST-segment elevation at the time of presentation, whereas the other eight developed ST changes during hospitalization. Nine patients underwent coronary angiography, and six were found to have an obstructive disease; five of these six patients needed percutaneous coronary intervention. Overall, eight patients were diagnosed as having an acute myocardial infarction, and the other ten were deemed to have a noncoronary myocardial injury. Of the 13 patients (72%) who passed away during hospitalization, four had a myocardial infarction, and the other nine had a noncoronary myocardial injury.**

**In Italy, researchers published a study of 28 patients with confirmed COVID-19 who had undergone with coronary angiogram for ST-elevation myocardial infarction. Of these, 79% had typical chest pain, while 21% presented with dyspnea without any chest pain; 86% had ST-elevation myocardial infarction as the initial presentation of COVID-19. This suggests that COVID-19 caused acute coronary syndrome (ACS) without substantial systemic inflammation. The pathophysiology of ACS in COVID-19 is not clear, but it may be related to direct endothelial**

**injury by the SARS-CoV-2 virus, microthrombi formation, or systemic inflammation and cytokine storm resulting in plaque rupture or coronary spasm.**

**Despite the association between COVID-19 and ACS, the reported incidence of ACS has been lower during the pandemic than in the pre-COVID-19 period. Reports indicate a 42%–48 % reduction in ACS hospitalizations and 38%–40% fewer percutaneous coronary interventions performed for ST-elevation myocardial infarction. This could be due to patients being reluctant to present to hospitals and clinics out of fear of contracting COVID-19. Unavailability of beds has also been a reason, as hospitals have been flooded with sick COVID-19 patients precluding many other admissions, particularly non-urgent cases.**

***We are very much thankful and great obliged for the inclusion of some part of the article here from COVID-19 and Cardiovascular Disease From Bench to Bedside by***

***Mina K. Chung,David A. Zidar,Michael R. Bristow,Scott J. Cameron,***

***Timothy Chan,Clifford V. Harding III,Deborah H. Kwon,Tamanna Singh,***

***John C. Tilton,Emily J. Tsai,Nathan R. Tucker,John Barnard andJoseph Loscalzo***

*Originally published15 Apr 2021*
*https://doi.org/10.1161/CIRCRESAHA.121.317997*
*Circulation Research. 2021; 128:1214–1236*

## *ACUTE CLINICAL MANIFESTATIONS*

## *(WHO DATA)*

**Patients with acute COVID-19 may present with a broad spectrum of clinical cardiac presentations: some patients manifest no clinical evidence of heart disease, some have no symptoms of heart disease but have cardiac test abnormalities (such as serum cardiac troponin elevation, asymptomatic cardiac arrhythmias, or abnormalities on cardiac imaging), and some have symptomatic heart disease. Cardiac complications include myocardial injury, heart failure (HF), cardiogenic shock, and cardiac arrhythmias including sudden cardiac arrest.**

**Most patients with COVID-19 with abnormalities on cardiac testing have typical symptoms of COVID-19, including cough, fever, myalgia, headache, and dyspnea, as described separately. A minority of patients with COVID-19 present with symptoms that may suggest heart disease (such as palpitations  or chest pain . These symptoms may or may not be accompanied by prior or concurrent symptoms typical of COVID-19 infection . Symptoms such as dyspnea and chest pain may be caused by noncardiac and/or cardiac causes.**

**Asymptomatic heart disease — Most patients with COVID-19 with cardiac test abnormalities (such as cardiac troponin elevation, electrocardiographic [ECG] abnormalities, or cardiac imaging findings) lack symptoms of heart disease.**

**As noted above, some symptoms, such as dyspnea, are nonspecific and are evaluated in the context of concurrent symptoms, signs, and test findings to determine if they are more likely caused by a noncardiac condition (eg, pneumonia) or cardiac disease.**

*Myocardial injury* **— Myocardial injury as detected by troponin elevation is commonly identified in patients hospitalized with COVID-19, but the causes of myocardial injury have not been fully elucidated . Cardiac troponin elevation does not distinguish among the causes of injury . There are many putative causes of myocardial injury in patients with COVID-19, but the cause in individual patients is frequently not identified. Clinical conditions associated with myocardial injury include myocarditis, stress cardiomyopathy, and myocardial infarction (MI).**

**The term "myocardial injury" encompasses all conditions causing cardiomyocyte death. Cardiac troponin elevation is the generally accepted marker for identifying myocardial injury . Myocardial injury is commonly clinically identified by the presence of at least one cardiac troponin value above the 99th percentile upper reference**

**limit (URL), in accordance with the definition of myocardial injury in the Fourth Universal Definition of Myocardial Infarction. While high-sensitivity cardiac troponin levels are sensitive markers of myocardial injury, some patients with disease processes causing cardiomyocyte death may have troponin levels below the 99th percentile URL .**

*Myocarditis* **— Numerous COVID-19 case reports have described findings consistent with a diagnosis of "clinically suspected myocarditis" , but there have been few cases of histologically confirmed myocarditis], and viral myocarditis caused directly by SARS-CoV-2 has not been definitively confirmed .**

**A potential association between mRNA vaccines to prevent SARS-CoV-2 infection and myocarditis is discussed here.**

*Stress cardiomyopathy* **— Stress (takotsubo) cardiomyopathy has been reported in patients with COVID-19 . In addition, some case reports of clinically suspected myocarditis complicating COVID-19 have described marked recovery of left ventricular (LV) systolic function within days, suggestive of stress cardiomyopathy or fulminant myocarditis.**

**In a review of 12 cases of stress cardiomyopathy associated with COVID-19, the mean age was 70.8 and the majority of patients were female. An elevated troponin level was**

**identified in 11 of the cases. There was no significant coronary artery disease on invasive coronary angiography in two patients, coronary artery disease in arteries supplying a different territory in one case, negative computed tomography coronary angiography in five cases, and no coronary artery disease on autopsy in one case; the coronary arteries were not examined in three cases. Complications included HF, cardiogenic shock, cardiac tamponade, and hypertensive crisis. Of note, a study identified increased incidence of stress cardiomyopathy in patients without COVID-19 during the COVID-19 pandemic.**

## Heart failure

## *(WHO DATA)*

**General prevalence — HF in patients with COVID-19 may be precipitated by acute illness in patients with preexisting known or undiagnosed heart disease (eg, coronary artery disease or hypertensive heart disease), acute hemodynamic stress (eg, acute cor pulmonale), or acute myocardial injury (eg, acute MI, stress cardiomyopathy, cytokine storm, and other possible etiologies described above). Cardiovascular risk factors and cardiovascular disease are highly prevalent in hospitalized patients with COVID-19. Patients with a known history of HF may suffer an acute decompensation due to the development of COVID-19 disease .**

**A study of 6439 patients hospitalized with COVID-19 at a hospital in New York found that a history of HF was associated with adverse outcomes, including longer length of stay (eight versus six days), increased risk of mechanical ventilation (22.8 versus 11.9 percent; adjusted odds ratio [OR] 3.64, 95% CI 2.56-5.16), and mortality (40.0 versus 24.9 percent; adjusted OR 1.88, 95% CI 1.27-2.78) . Outcomes among patients with different types of HF were similar, regardless of LV ejection fraction (LVEF).**

**Limited data are available on the incidence of HF in patients with COVID-19.**

**Although acute HF incidence was not documented in some series of hospitalized patients with COVID-19, elevated natriuretic peptides (such as B-type natriuretic peptide [BNP] and N-terminal pro-BNP [NT-proBNP]) are common, particularly in patients with evidence of cardiac injury.**

**Right heart failure — Acute cor pulmonale (right HF due to acute pulmonary hypertension) precipitated by acute pulmonary embolism or adult respiratory distress syndrome (ARDS) has been described in patients with COVID-19 . Patients with COVID-19 are at risk for development of ARDS. Venous thromboembolism (including extensive deep vein thrombosis and pulmonary embolism) is common in acutely ill patients with COVID-19. Cardiogenic shock — Case reports have described**

**patients with COVID-19 and acute onset of cardiogenic shock treated with inotrope and mechanical circulatory support and, in some cases, venoarterial extracorporeal membrane oxygenation (VA-ECMO) . Rapid recovery within several days has been described in several reported cases with a time course suggestive of possible stress cardiomyopathy . Although fulminant myocarditis was suspected in some cases of cardiogenic shock with recovery of ventricular function over days or weeks, this diagnosis has generally not been established, as endomyocardial biopsy was either not performed or, when performed, did not show findings of myocarditil.**

**Multisystem inflammatory syndrome in adults (MIS-A) — Multisystem inflammatory syndrome (MIS) was initially described in children (MIS-C) with recent COVID-19 infection as a Kawasaki-like illness associated with fever, gastrointestinal symptoms, shock, LV systolic dysfunction, and elevated inflammatory markers.**

**Similar cases of MIS have been described in young to middle-aged adults (MIS-A) also presenting with fever, gastrointestinal symptoms, and shock with vasoplegia, LV systolic dysfunction, and elevated inflammatory markers . Many of these patients had history of recent COVID-19 and had positive SARS-CoV-2 antibody tests, with fewer having positive SARS-CoV-2 reverse transcription polymerase chain reaction tests. This diagnosis should be considered in young adults presenting with shock and**

**elevated inflammatory markers. This syndrome appears to be highly responsive to parenteral steroids.**

*Cardiac arrhythmias* **— The risk of cardiac arrhythmias and sudden cardiac arrest in patients with COVID-19 is observed. CARDIAC TEST FINDINGS is variety of cardiac test abnormalities have been done in patients with COVID-19.**

*Biomarkers* **— Cardiac troponin and natriuretic peptide (B-type natriuretic peptide [BNP] and N-terminal pro-BNP [NT-proBNP]) biomarkers are commonly elevated among hospitalized patients with COVID-19 and are associated with increased risk of mortality. In a study from Wuhan of 3219 patients (mean age 57 years) with COVID-19 hospitalized with biomarker data, elevated high-sensitivity cardiac troponin I (hs-cTnI) was detected in 6.5 percent, and an elevated NT-proBNP level was detected in 12.9 percent . In a model including adjustment for age, sex, and comorbidities, the adjusted hazard ratio for 28-day mortality for hs-cTnI was 7.12 (95% CI 4.60-11.03) and for NT-proBNP was 5.11 (95% CI 3.50-7.47). These biomarkers had prognostic value at approximately half of the commonly used upper limit of normal thresholds.**

**A similar association between biomarker elevation and mortality risk was observed in a study from Milan in Italy of 397 hospitalized patients with COVID-19 . At the time of hospital admission, 22.7 percent had elevated hs-cTnI**

**and BNP levels, 14.9 percent had only an elevated BNP level, and 10.1 percent had only an elevated hs-cTnI. Overall mortality rate was 23.2 percent. The mortality rate was higher in patients with elevation of both biomarkers (55.6 percent), elevated BNP (33.9 percent), or hs-cTnI elevation (22.5 percent) compared with patients with no biomarker elevation (6.25 percent). In multivariate analysis, elevation of both hs-cTnI and BNP was an independent predictor of mortality (odds ratio [OR] 3.24, 95% CI 1.06-9.93).**

*Troponin* **— Cardiac troponin elevation is a marker of myocardial injury and is commonly identified in patients hospitalized with COVID-19, but the causes of troponin elevation have not been fully elucidated . The frequency of myocardial injury (as reflected by elevation in cardiac troponin levels) is variable among hospitalized patients with COVID-19, with reported frequencies of 7 to 36 percent. The frequency of troponin elevation appears to be lower among patients with mildly symptomatic COVID-19 . Frequencies of troponin elevation in various COVID-19 series are difficult to compare due to use of differing troponin assays, 99th percentile upper reference limit (URL) thresholds, and sampling times. Limited data are available on the frequency of troponin elevations in asymptomatic or only mildly symptomatic patients with SARS-CoV-2 infection.**

**Studies have identified greater frequency and magnitude of troponin elevations in hospitalized patients with more severe disease and worse outcomes. A systematic review and meta-analysis found that an elevated troponin level was among the clinical factors most strongly associated with an adverse composite outcome (including death, severe presentation, hospitalization in the intensive care unit, and/or mechanical ventilation; OR 10.58, 95% CI 5.00-22.40) . Other clinical features associated with high risk of the composite outcomes were history of cardiovascular disease, acute kidney injury, increased nonreciprocal, increased D-dimer, and thrombolytic. An elevated tronning level was also one of the clinical features associated with in-hospital death.**

**In a study from New York of 2736 hospitalized patients (mean age 66.4 years) with COVID-19, 36 percent of patients had elevated hs-cTnI levels [69]. Troponin elevation was more prevalent among patients with known cardiovascular disease or cardiovascular risk factors. The mortality rate during hospitalization was 18.5 percent. In adjusted analysis, even mildly elevated hs-cTnI (0.03 to 0.09 ng/mL) was associated with risk of death (adjusted hazard ratio [HR] 1.75, 95% CI 1.37-2.24), while greater elevations were associated with higher risk (troponin >0.09 ng/mL; adjusted HR 3.03, 95% CI 2.42-3.80).**

**In a series of 416 patients with COVID-19 who were hospitalized at Renmin Hospital in Wuhan, 19.7 percent**

**had hs-cTnI above the 99th percentile URL on admission [11]. Patients with this marker of myocardial injury were older and had more comorbidities (including chronic HF in 14.6 versus 1.5 percent), greater laboratory abnormalities (including higher levels of C-reactive protein, procalcitonin, and aspartate aminotransferase), more lung radiographic abnormalities, and more complications compared with those without myocardial injury. The mortality rate was also higher in those with myocardial injury (51.2 versus 4.5 percent). The risk of death starting from the time of symptom onset was more than four times higher in patients with evidence of myocardial injury on admission (HR 4.26, 95% CI 1.92-9.49).**

**In a study from Wuhan of 311 hospitalized patients with COVID-19 and available hs-cTnI levels, independent risk factors for death included hs-cTnI concentration (OR 1.92, 95% CI 1.41-2.59), comorbidity (OR 9.07, 95% CI 2.52-32.66), C-reactive protein concentration (OR 1.98, 95% CI 1.34-2.92), D-dimer concentration (OR 1.55, 95% CI 1.13-2.13), lymphocyte count (OR 0.52, 95% CI 0.29-0.95), and blood oxygen saturation (OR 0.85, 95% CI 0.77-0.94).**

**In another study from Wuhan, elevation in hs-cTnI above the 99th percentile URL was identified on admission in 46 percent of non survivors versus 1 percent of survivors . In contrast, a study of 24 critically ill COVID-19 patients in Seattle with a 50 percent mortality rate found elevated**

**troponin levels early after intensive care unit admission in only 2 of 13 (15 percent) tested patients, but troponin assays may have differed . A study found considerably greater prevalence of preexisting cardiovascular disease and cardiac risk factors in patients with evidence of myocardial injury compared with those without elevated biomarkers . Thus, it is not yet possible to determine whether myocardial injury is an independent risk marker in COVID-19 or if the risk associated with it is related to the burden of preexisting cardiovascular disease.**

**In patients with COVID-19, troponin elevation may be initially detected prior to, at the time of, or following hospital admission [25-28,54,65,67,74]. A variety of time courses for troponin elevation have been observed:**

- **Mild – Patients hospitalized with COVID-19 commonly have mild troponin elevation (typically <99th percentile URL), with modest rise or fall on subsequent days, typically remaining well below the 99th percentile URL . This appears to be the most common pattern of troponin elevation in patients with COVID-19 and is often associated with no cardiac symptoms. This pattern has been described in patients with COVID-19 who survived after hospitalization .**
- **Moderate time-limited – Some patients have an early moderately elevated troponin level (which may approach or exceed the 99th percentile URL), which may fall on subsequent days. This pattern was seen in**

**anecdotal reports of patients with clinically suspected myocarditis or stress cardiomyopathy**

**•Progressive – Some patients with moderate troponin elevation at hospital admission suffer clinical deterioration with respiratory failure accompanied by progressive troponin elevation, along with elevations in other biomarkers (eg, D-dimer, interleukin , ferritin, and lactate dehydrogenase) with accelerated rise after the second week of hospitalization . This progression to cytokine storm has been described in nonsurvivors, with death occurring at a median of 18.5 days after symptom onset.**

**Other cardiac test abnormalities (such as ECG alterations and cardiac imaging findings) have been observed in patients with and without elevated troponin levels. The finding of a cardiac test abnormality without concurrent troponin elevation suggests a condition not associated with myocardial injury (including preexisting cardiac disease or a process not causing cardiomyocyte death) or a missed troponin level elevation due to limited troponin sampling or troponin elevation below 99th percentile URL thresholds**

*Natriuretic peptides* **— Natriuretic peptides (BNP and NT-proBNP) are commonly elevated in hospitalized patients with COVID-19, and natriuretic peptide elevation is associated with mortality risk.**

**Natriuretic peptide elevation is commonly associated with cardiac troponin elevation. In the above described series of 416 hospitalized patients with COVID-19, NT-proBNP levels were significantly higher in patients with elevated troponin levels than in patients without troponin elevation (1689 versus 139 pg/mL) .**

*Electrocardiogram:*

**The various ECG findings observed in patients with COVID-19 likely reflect the combined effects of acute illness and chronic heart disease (since cardiovascular risk factors are highly prevalent in this population). The range of ECG findings was illustrated in a study of 756 patients (mean age 63 years) hospitalized with COVID-19 in New York . The mortality rate was 11.9 percent during the follow-up period of two to seven weeks. Cardiovascular risk factors and conditions were common, including obesity (37 percent), diabetes mellitus (29 percent), hypertension (57 percent), coronary artery disease (CAD, 14 percent) and HF (7 percent). This study did not include data on troponin levels or comparison with prior ECGs.**

- **Atrial fibrillation or flutter was observed in 5.6 percent. Atrial premature beats (APBs) were observed in 7.7 percent and premature ventricular contractions in 3.4 percent.**

- **Right bundle branch block (RBBB) was identified in 7.8 percent, left bundle branch block in 1.5 percent, and nonspecific intraventricular conduction delay (IVCD) in 2.5 percent.**
- **Repolarization abnormalities included localized ST elevation in 0.7 percent, localized T-wave inversion in 10.5 percent, and nonspecific repolarization abnormalities in 29 percent.**
- **In a multivariable model including age, clinical characteristics, and ECG findings, the variables associated with risk of death were presence of CAD, an immunosuppressed state, hypoxemia, and the following ECG findings: APBs (OR 2.57, 95% CI 1.23-5.36), RBBB or IVCD (OR 2.61, 95% CI 1.32-5.18), localized T-wave inversion (OR 3.49, 95% CI 1.56-7.80), and nonspecific repolarization abnormality (OR 2.31, 95% CI 1.27-4.21).**

*Cardiac imagingEchocardiogram* **— A variety of echocardiographic findings have been identified in patients with COVID-19 , as illustrated by a study of an unselected population of 100 patients hospitalized with COVID-19 .**

- **Transthoracic echocardiography (TTE) findings included right ventricular (RV) dilation and dysfunction (39 percent), LV diastolic dysfunction (16 percent), and LV systolic dysfunction (10 percent). Patients with an elevated troponin level or worse clinical condition had worse RV function.**

- **Among the 20 percent of patients with subsequent clinical deterioration, the most common echocardiographic findings were worsened RV function (12 patients) and worsened LV systolic and diastolic function (5 patients). Femoral deep vein thrombosis was identified in 5 of 12 patients with RV failure.**

**The spectrum of findings in patients with COVID-19 with a clinical indication for TTE was illustrated by an international survey including data on 1216 patients (mean age 62) from 69 countries:**

- **The most common indications for TTE were suspected left-sided HF (40 percent), elevated cardiac biomarkers (26 percent), and right-sided HF (20 percent). Preexisting heart disease was noted in 26 percent of patients.**
- **Fifty-five percent of patients had an abnormal TTE, including LV abnormalities in 39 percent and RV abnormalities is 33 percent. A slightly lower prevalence of echocardiographic abnormalities (46 percent) was detected in the subgroup of patients with no known preexisting heart disease.**
- **TTE LV findings were considered suggestive of diagnoses including acute MI (3 percent), myocarditis (3 percent), and stress cardiomyopathy (3 percent). Severe ventricular (left, right, or biventricular) dysfunction was observed in 14 percent. Cardiac tamponade was identified in 1 percent.**

- **TTE findings changed management in 33 percent of patients.**

**The prognostic importance of major TTE abnormalities was demonstrated by a study of 305 patients (mean age 63 years) who had undergone TTE during hospitalization for COVID-19 [80]. Troponin elevation was observed in 62.3 percent of these patients. Patients with troponin elevation had more ECG abnormalities and higher prevalence of major TTE abnormalities (including LV wall motion abnormalities, global LV dysfunction, LV diastolic dysfunction grade II or III, RV dysfunction, and pericardial effusions) than patients without troponin elevation. Rates of in-hospital mortality were 5.2 percent in patients without myocardial injury, 18.6 in those with myocardial injury without TTE abnormalities, and 31.7 percent in patients with myocardial injury and TTE abnormalities. Following multi variable adjustment, myocardial injury with TTE abnormalities was associated with higher risk of death, but myocardial injury without TTE abnormalities was not.**

***Cardiovascular magnetic resonance*** **— Cardiovascular magnetic resonance (CMR) abnormalities have been identified in patients with COVID-19 as well as in patients who have recently recovered from COVID-19, though most reported abnormalities have been nonspecific. CMR findings identified in some of these patients include elevations in native T1 (a nonspecific finding seen with**

**acute myocardial injury, fibrosis, or infiltration), T2 (a marker of edema), and, less commonly, late gadolinium enhancement (a marker of acute myocardial injury, fibrosis, or infarction). Since limited endo myocardial biopsy data and no follow-up data have been reported, the clinical significance of these findings is uncertain. Moreover, since no patients had a CMR examination before COVID-19, it remains undetermined whether the abnormal findings might have already been present and therefore be unrelated to COVID-19.**

- **In an selected cohort – A CMR study included 100 patients (mean age 49 years) who had recovered from COVID-19, including 18 with asymptomatic SARS-CoV-2 infection, 49 with mild to moderate symptoms, and 33 with severe symptoms requiring hospitalization . Preexisting cardiovascular conditions such as hypertension, diabetes mellifluous, and known coronary artery disease were equally common among patients who remained at home and those who were hospitalized. Patients referred for CMR for cardiac symptoms were excluded. Comparisons were made with healthy controls as well as with risk factor-matched controls.**
  - **Among the 33 hospitalized patients, 15 patients had a significantly elevated hs-cTnI during hospitalization. Among all the patients, 5 percent has significant hs-cTnI elevation at the time of CMR. CMR was**

**performed two to three months after the initial positive COVID-19 test.**

**•Abnormal CMR findings were frequent among those who had recovered from COVID-19, including elevated myocardial native T1 (73 percent), elevated myocardial native T2 (60 percent), myocardial late gadolinium enhancement (LGE; 32 percent), and pericardial LGE (22 percent). Baseline CMR data were not available.**

**-In healthy controls, T1 and T2 elevations were rare and LGE was not seen.**

**-In risk-factor matched controls, CMR abnormalities were identified, although at lower frequencies than in the COVID-19 group: elevated native T1 (40 percent), elevated native T2 (9 percent), myocardial LGE (17 percent), and pericardial LGE (15 percent).**

**•Endomyocardial biopsy in three patients with elevated hs-cTnI, elevated native T1 and T2, LGE, and LVEF <50 percent revealed lymphocytic infiltration; necrosis was not described and no viral genome was detected.**

**•The LV was mildly dilated and LVEF and RVEF were mildly depressed in patients recovered from COVID-19 compared with healthy controls and risk-factor matched controls (for LVEF 56 versus 60 and 61 percent, respectively; for RVEF 56 versus 60 and 59 percent).**

**•In athletes – CMR findings have also been reported among athletes who have recovered from COVID-19 . The clinical significance of these findings is uncertain since CMR findings are nonspecific and endomyocardial biopsy data were not reported. Studies have identified CMR findings including LGE in a minority of healthy adult athletes with no prior COVID-19 infection [86-89]:**

- **•Collegiate athletes – After small studies identified CMR abnormalities in collegiate athletes recovering from COVID-19, a larger study found that CMR findings consistent with clinically suspected myocarditis were rare. In a study of 145 university student athletes (mean age 20 years; 74 percent male), CMR examination was performed at a median of 15 days after the positive COVID-19 tests . Most patients experienced mild, moderate, or no symptoms during the acute COVID-19 infection. Two patients (1.4 percent) had findings consistent with updated Lake Louise criteria for clinically suspected myocarditis (see "Clinical manifestations and diagnosis of myocarditis in adults", section on 'Updated Lake Louise criteria'). One of these patients had patchy midmyocardial and subepicardial LGE with associated elevated T2-weighted signal, transient troponin I elevation, and pericardial enhancement. CMR examination of the second patient revealed a 1 cm focus of mild epicardial LGE at the inferior basal**

**LV wall with corresponding elevated T2-weighted signal; an additional small nonspecific LGE focus was identified at the inferior RV insertion. No endomyocardial biopsy data were available. 40 patients (27.6 percent) had small nonspecific foci of LGE.**

**In a study that recorded the one-year incidence of CV disease among almost 5.8 million United States veterans, patients who had COVID-19 had an increased risk of death or major adverse CV events (eg, stroke, MI, arrhythmia, HF) when compared with a group of patients who did not have COVID-19 (23 excess CV events per 1000 patients with COVID-19; adjusted hazard ratio 1.55, 95% CI 1.5-1.6) . In addition, patients hospitalized with more severe COVID-19 (ie, hospitalized for COVID-19) were more likely to develop CV disease when compared with patients with less severe COVID-19.**

## Potential bias and chance:

**Some critics of the recent preprint say that choosing to analyze BsaI and BsmBI and not other restriction sites was biased, and would lead to skewed results.**

**However, Washburne said that the authors chose BsaI and BsmBI because their regular pattern stood out right away. Restriction sites ideal for engineering are evenly spaced along the genome to provide genomic fragments of similar**

**lengths, while naturally occuring sites are usually randomly scattered throughout the genome.**

**Bruttel added that "most other type IIS enzymes just cannot be combined or produce shorter sticky ends."**

**Longer ends can make assembly easier.**

**BsaI and BsmBI are also two of the most commonly used restriction**

**for the assembling viral genomes.**

***Two labs that employed BsaI and BsmI to cut coronaviruses include the Wuhan Institute of Virology, which used the restriction sites to swap spike proteins, and the Baric Lab at the University of North Carolina, which used the restriction sites to reconstruct SARS-CoV-2 in 2020*.**

**Critics of the preprint also say that the seemingly unusual restriction site map observed by the authors could have occurred naturally, either by silent mutations or recombination. Silent mutations alter DNA without changing any encoded proteins, while recombination happens when two different genomes swap segments of DNA.**

**The microbiologists concede that recombination could explain the unusual restriction map, but that it could also**

**make their results more significant and that more research on this is needed.**

**The microbiologists also argue that silent mutations are an unlikely explanation for SARS-CoV-2's unusual restriction map.**

**"Microbiologists find exceptionally many (and only silent) mutations occur in the tiny part of the genome that make up these restriction sites," says Bruttel.**

**Such a high rate of silent mutations in the restriction sites is unlikely to occur naturally, and "indicates that they were manipulated," he added.**

**The preprint attracted ridicule from prominent proponents of the zoonosis theory.**

**"Pure unadulterated nonsense. … This paper will never be published," Vincent Racaniello, a Columbia University virologist, said in an email.**

**Scripps Research Institute virologist Kristian Andersen excoriated the preprint as failing "kindergarten molecular biology" in a viral tweet thread.**

**After the preprint was released, Andersen said that he too had examined SARS-CoV-2 restriction sites in late January and early February of 2020 — around the time he**

**presented his suspicions that the virus was engineered to a group of top virologists and leaders of the NIH.**

**Andersen shared the results of his analysis on Twitter, which he claimed indicated that BsaI and BsmI restriction sites appear to occur naturally along similar places in the genome of related viruses.**

**Zoonosis proponents' worries about the Baric Lab**

**Concerns about whether in vitro genetic assembly methods on coronaviruses employed by the Baric Lab and the Wuhan Institute of Virology could have factored into the origin of COVID-19 are not new.**

**As the pandemic first picked up speed in January and February 2020, National Institutes of Health (NIH) leaders and top virologists, including Andersen, fretted over a controversial gain-of-function experiment conducted by the Baric Lab and the Wuhan Institute of Virology which assembled chimeric SARS-like coronavirus genomes using different restriction sites.**

**The scientists were concerned that the methods described in the paper outlined "a how-to manual for building the Wuhan coronavirus in a laboratory."**

*It has been found that some individuals persistently test positive for the virus even longer time after clearing the infection. This is important because it's not clear whether such individuals have been re-infected or whether they continue to be infectious to others. So-called 'human genome invasion' by SARS-CoV-2 has been suggested as an explanation for this observation.*

*If the virus was able to integrate its genetic material into the human genome, that could have meant that any other mRNA could do the same. It is possible for the genetic material of some viruses to be incorporated into the DNA of humans and other animals, resulting in what scientists call "chimeric events." Human DNA contains approximately 100,000 pieces of DNA from viruses that our species have accumulated over millions of years of evolution. In total, this lost-and-found DNA from viruses makes up a bit less than 10% of the genetic material in our cells.*

*Virologists have shown that the SARS-CoV-2 virus can also cause these chimeric events. Even before this new research team conducted experiments showing this was not the case, the researchers suspected it was unlikely, said Dr. Ben Afzali, an Earl Stadtman Investigator of the National Institutes of Health's National Institute of Diabetes and Digestive and Kidney Diseases and a co-lead author on the study.*

*"While an earlier study suggested that, in cells infected with SARS-CoV-2, genetic material from the virus copied and pasted itself into human DNA, our group thought this seemed unlikely," Afzali said. "SARS-CoV-2, like HIV, has its genetic material in the form of RNA but, unlike HIV, does not have the*

*machinery to convert the RNA into DNA. SARS-CoV-2 is unlikely to paste itself into the genome and corona-viruses, in general, does not go near human DNA. It is highly improbable that SARS-CoV-2 could integrate into the human genome.*

*Christiane Wobus, associate professor of microbiology and immunology at the University of Michigan Medical School, also a co-lead author on the study, said that although the collective understanding of RNA viruses is that integration of SARS-CoV-2 into the human genome would be very unlikely.*

*"Unexpected findings in science — when confirmed independently — lead to paradigm shifts and propel fields forward. Therefore, it is good to be open-minded and examine unexpected results carefully. To examine the proposed integration event, the Microbiologists developed a novel technique in which they extracted the genetic material from infected cells and then amplified or reproduced the genetic material 30-fold. If there were chimeric events in the host cell DNA, these bits of genetic material from SARS-CoV-2 should also increase 30 times. The data did not show this.*

*Gene editing*

*Each organism has a unique genetic code which is determined by the sequence of the DNA chemical letters, C, G, A and T. A section of code that is responsible for a specific characteristic is known as a gene. These sections of code can vary from a few hundred letters to over a million depending on the gene. Genome editing is the process of changing the genetic code of an organism by inserting, deleting, modifying or replacing sections of DNA. Gene editing uses specialised tools to cut away a section of DNA at a specific site and sometimes insert a new section. This can be employed to mend DNA This can be employed to mend DNA by correcting mutations that cause disease, to insert entirely new bits of DNA giving an organism new characteristics, or to discover the function of specific genes.*

*Gene editing has already been performed on animals, plants, bacteria and even humans, but it is still in its infancy. However, recent discoveries, such as CRISPR/Cas9, have made it cheaper, quicker and more accurate. Cas9 is an enzyme that has the ability to cut DNA, which is often likened to 'molecular scissors'. It is guided to the correct place by 'guide RNA', which is similar to DNA, and has the ability to stick to a section of DNA if its genetic code is complementary. By designing the guide RNA to stick to a gene of interest we can guide Cas9 to cut the DN use the natural DNA repair mechanisms of the cell to insert a new gene or reconnect the DNA where a gene has been removed. The CRISPR/Cas9 system enables cheap and rapid editing of genes with Mosquitoes have the ability to carry and transmit many deadly diseases that are responsible for millions of deaths and billions of pounds of economic losses every year, particularly in developing countries. Pirbright carries out research to understand how genetically modified mosquitoes can be used for the control of mosquito populations to prevent diseases of both livestock and people.*

*One of the most promising control techniques is known as a gene drive. This is where the mosquito genome is modified to decrease their ability to breed or carry infections, and this modification is favourable spread into a population at a faster rate than normal inheritance. As these modified mosquitoes mate with the wild population, up to 100% of the next generation inherit the modification whereas normal inheritance would give only up to 50%. This means the number of modified mosquitoes that need to be released to make an effective change to the population is much lower than other strategies. Researchers in the Arthropod Genetics group are particularly interested in developing safe, reversible gene drive designs that will modify a target mosquito population but remain local in their effect.*

## *FURIN*

*Furin is a protein found in humans and animals which can be exploited by viruses like coronavirus, HIV and Ebola to help them spread by activating the proteins which hold the virus, and are contained in "cleavage sites". (REF.*)*

*The study said the "furin-like cleavage site" in SARS-CoV-2 "may provide a gain-of-function to the 2019-nCov for efficient spreading in the human population" compared to other coronaviruses.*

*In simple terms, this means that the presence of this site in the virus could be the reason why it is infecting so many people. However, the study makes absolutely no suggestion that the virus has been "genetically engineered" to cause this.*

*We spoke to the Science Media Centre who asked experts what they made of the paper's claim.*

*Professor Ben Neuman, chair of biological sciences at Texas A&M University-Texarkana and visiting associate professor at the University of Reading, said: "The Daily Express's take is not based on science and appears to be rather inflammatory."*

*"All the furin-like cleavage site tells us is that this virus probably comes from another animal with a furin-like enzyme in its lungs, which includes pretty much any mammal or bird that you could name.*

*"The paper makes no such claim about tampering—it is referring to the process of evolution in general."*

*Professor Wendy Barclay, chair in influenza virology at Imperial College London, said there is "convergent evolution" present in SARS-Cov-2 but "by genetic engineering design there's just no way scientists would have known how to achieve this."*

*"The [Express] article has not really gone into the science in a way that can give the balanced argument," she said, adding that most data so far "strongly support the idea that the novel coronavirus emerged through natural recombination and evolution of coronaviruses of bats."*

*Dr Michael Skinner, reader in virology at Imperial College London, said experts "recognise this kind of mutation as common in the natural evolution of viruses", particularly those like coronaviruses.*

*CRISPR -Cas9:*

**CRISPR is an acronym for Clustered Regularly Interspaced Short Palindromic Repeat. This name refers to the unique organization of short, partially palindromic repeated DNA sequences found in the genomes of bacteria**

**and other microorganisms. While seemingly innocuous, CRISPR sequences are a crucial component of the immune systems of these simple life forms. The immune system is responsible for protecting an organism's health and well-being. Just like us, bacterial cells can be invaded by viruses, which are small, infectious agents. If a viral infection threatens a bacterial cell, the CRISPR immune system can thwart the attack by destroying the genome of the invading virus . The genome of the virus includes genetic material that is necessary for the virus to continue replicating. Thus, by destroying the viral genome, the CRISPR immune system protects bacteria from ongoing viral infection. CRISPRs are regions in the bacterial genome that help defend against invading viruses. These regions are composed of short DNA repeats (black diamonds) and spacers (colored boxes). When a previously unseen virus infects a bacterium, a new spacer derived from the virus is incorporated among st existing spacers. The CRISPR sequence is transcribed and processed to generate short CRISPR RNA molecules. The CRISPR RNA associates with and guides bacterial molecular machinery to a matching target sequence in the invading virus. The molecular machinery cuts up and destroys the invading viral genome. It has been shown from Molecular Cell 54, April 24, 2014 .Interspersed between the short DNA repeats of bacterial CRISPRs are similarly short variable sequences called spacers . These spacers are derived from DNA of viruses that have previously attacked**

**the host bacterium [3]. Hence, spacers serve as a 'genetic memory' of previous infections. If another infection by the same virus should occur, the CRISPR defense system will cut up any viral DNA sequence matching the spacer sequence and thus protect the bacterium from viral attack. If a previously unseen virus attacks, a new spacer is made and added to the chain of spacers and repeats.**

**The CRISPR immune system works to protect bacteria from repeated viral attack via three basic steps :**

**Step 1) Adaptation – DNA from an invading virus is processed into short segments that are inserted into the CRISPR sequence as new spacers.**

**Step 2) Production of CRISPR RNA – CRISPR repeats and spacers in the bacterial DNA undergo transcription, the process of copying DNA into RNA (ribonucleic acid). Unlike the double-chain helix structure of DNA, the resulting RNA is a single-chain molecule. This RNA chain is cut into short pieces called CRISPR RNAs.**

**Step 3) Targeting – CRISPR RNAs guide bacterial molecular machinery to destroy the viral material. Because CRISPR RNA sequences are copied from the viral DNA sequences acquired during adaptation, they are exact matches to the viral genome and thus serve as excellent guides.**

**The specificity of CRISPR-based immunity in recognizing and destroying invading viruses is not just useful for bacteria. Creative applications of this primitive yet elegant defense system have emerged in disciplines as diverse as industry, basic research, and medicine.**

*Applications of the CRISPR system*

**(i) In Industry**

**The inherent functions of the CRISPR system are advantageous for industrial processes that utilize bacterial cultures. CRISPR-based immunity can be employed to make these cultures more resistant to viral attack, which would otherwise impede productivity. In fact, the original discovery of CRISPR immunity came from researchers at Danisco, a company in the food production industry. Danisco scientists were studying a bacterium called Streptococcus thermophilus, which is used to make yogurts and cheeses. Certain viruses can infect this bacterium and damage the quality or quantity of the food. It was discovered that CRISPR sequences equipped S. thermophilus with immunity against such viral attack. Expanding beyond S. thermophilus to other useful bacteria, manufacturers can apply the same principles to improve culture sustainability and lifespan.**

**(ii) In the Lab**

**Beyond applications encompassing bacterial immune defenses, scientists have learned how to harness CRISPR technology in the lab [6] to make precise changes in the genes of organisms as diverse as fruit flies, fish, mice, plants and even human cells. Genes are defined by their specific sequences, which provide instructions on how to build and maintain an organism's cells. A change in the sequence of even one gene can significantly affect the biology of the cell and in turn may affect the health of an organism. CRISPR techniques allow scientists to modify specific genes while sparing all others, thus clarifying the association between a given gene and its consequence to the organism.**

**Rather than relying on bacteria to generate CRISPR RNAs, scientists first design and synthesize short RNA molecules that match a specific DNA sequence—for example, in a human cell. Then, like in the targeting step of the bacterial system, this 'guide RNA' shuttles molecular machinery to the intended DNA target. Once localized to the DNA region of interest, the molecular machinery can silence a gene or even change the sequence of a gene This type of gene editing can be likened to editing a sentence with a word processor to delete words or correct spelling mistakes. One important application of such technology is to facilitate making animal models with precise genetic changes to study the progress and treatment of human diseases.**

## Gene silencing and editing with CRISPR.

**Guide RNA designed to match the DNA region of interest directs molecular machinery to cut both strands of the targeted DNA. During gene silencing, the cell attempts to repair the broken DNA, but often does so with errors that disrupt the gene—effectively silencing it. For gene editing, a repair template with a specified change in sequence is added to the cell and incorporated into the DNA during the repair process. The targeted DNA is now altered to carry this new sequence.**

### (iii) In Medicine

**With early successes in the lab, many are looking toward medical applications of CRISPR technology. One application is for the treatment of genetic diseases. The first evidence that CRISPR can be used to correct a mutant gene and reverse disease symptoms in a living animal was published earlier this year [REF,*]. By replacing the mutant form of a gene with its correct sequence in adult mice, researchers demonstrated a cure for a rare liver disorder that could be achieved with a single treatment. In addition to treating heritable diseases, CRISPR can be used in the realm of infectious diseases, possibly providing a way to make more specific antibiotics**

**that target only disease-causing bacterial strains while sparing beneficial bacteria [8]. A recent SITN Waves article discusses how this technique was also used to make white blood cells resistant to HIV infection .**

## (iv) The Future of CRISPR

**Of course, any new technology takes some time to understand and perfect. It will be important to verify that a particular guide RNA is specific for its target gene, so that the CRISPR system does not mistakenly attack other genes. It will also be important to find a way to deliver CRISPR therapies into the body before they can become widely used in medicine. Although a lot remains to be discovered, there is no doubt that CRISPR has become a valuable tool in research. In fact, there is enough excitement in the field to warrant the launch of several Biotech start-ups that hope to use CRISPR-inspired technology to treat human diseases.** ***We are highly obliged and gratefully acknowledge some portions Taken here from THESIS PART OF Ekaterina Pak , a Ph.D. student in the Biological and Biomedical Sciences program at Harvard Medical School*, U.S.A.**

**References:**

**1. Palca, J. A CRISPR way to fix faulty genes. (26 June 2014) NPR**

**< http://www.npr.org/blogs/health/2014/06/26/325213397/a-crispr-way-to-fix-faulty-genes> [29 June 2014]**

**2. Pennisi, E. The CRISPR Craze. (2013) Science, 341 (6148): 833-836.**

**3. Barrangou, R., Fremaux, C., Deveau, H., Richards, M., Boyaval, P., Moineau, S., Romero, D.A., and Horvath, P. (2007). CRISPR provides acquired resistance against viruses in prokaryotes. Science 315, 1709–1712.**

**4. Brouns, S.J., Jore, M.M., Lundgren, M., Westra,**

**A NEW, HIGHLY transmissible strain of influenza emerges. A pesticide-resistant insect decimates huge swaths of crops. A patient winds up in the emergency room with a bacterial strain that doesn't respond to any available antibiotics. Any of these scenarios could happen due to natural evolutionary changes among pathogens or pests. But as genetic engineering gets cheaper and easier, it's becoming increasingly plausible that they might one day be the product of deliberate manipulation.To guard against these potential threats, the US government is funding the development of tests to detect dangerous bioengineered organisms before they have a chance to cause significant harm. The effort was announced in 2017 by the Intelligence Advanced Research Projects Activity, or Iarpa, within the Office of the Director of National**

**Intelligence. In a live streamed update in October, Iarpa program manager David Markowitz announced that two platforms developed under the program were both 70 percent accurate at identifying the presence of bioengineering. “We simply never know what sample is going to come through the door in a government lab, and we need to be prepared for anything,” Markowitz said during the news briefing. One of the platforms, created by the nonprofit Draper, based in Cambridge, Massachusetts, is a rapid, handheld testing device that uses a thumbnail-sized chip to detect engineered genetic material. The other is software developed by Boston biotech company Ginkgo Bioworks that uses machine learning to identify engineering in genomic data generated from sample organisms. (The companies haven’t yet published their results in a peer-reviewed journal, and their platforms are still in development.)**

**Crops and animal feed are already widely screened to determine the presence of genetic traits that can’t be found in nature or created through conventional breeding. Scientists use a test called PCR, or polymer chain reaction, to identify whether bio-engineered DNA is present and in what amount. When it comes to food labeling, scientists usually know what genetic change they’re looking for. But no general-purpose tool exists for detecting engineered genetic material in bacteria, viruses, or other organisms that could appear in any context.**

**Until now, detecting the presence of bioengineering relied on manual analysis, which is labor-intensive and slow. Through a process called sequencing, researchers can generate a readout of an organism's entire genetic code: a series of As, Cs, Gs, and Ts, or bases, which make up the building blocks of life. Every microbe, plant, animal, and human has a unique configuration of these letters.To determine whether an organism's genetic code has been tinkered with, scientists need to know what its genome—and those of its close relatives—normally look like. Then they can search for areas that look out of the ordinary.**

**DNA can be manipulated through at least a half dozen processes. A conventional method involves adding a gene from one species to another—usually for bioengineering crops. Chunks of DNA can also be moved from one part of an organism's genome to another part, a type of change called a translocation. Crispr gene editing, which is being explored as a way to treat diseases in people, and to improve plants and animals bred for human consumption, can delete chunks of DNA. Older editing techniques, such as zinc finger nucleases and Talens, have also been used for these purposes but haven't been as successful as Crispr.**

**Any of these processes may leave behind signatures of bioengineering. For example, scientists can tell if a gene has been added or moved by comparing that organism's genome to a reference sample. When using Crispr, deletions sometimes turn up in other parts of the genome that look like the targeted section, but aren't. Talens and zinc finger nucleases also have a tendency to produce these "off-target" effects. The deliberate use of radiation can also produce traceable DNA mutations.**

**Draper and Ginkgo's technologies are designed to detect these common signatures of engineering. Ginkgo's software also relies on algorithms that compare the genome being analyzed against those in a huge database to determine whether it looks like an engineered or natural one. Draper's device is meant to be deployed quickly in the field on single samples, while Ginkgo's is designed to do large-scale analysis of many samples.**

**"Genetic engineering has been happening for quite a while now, and it's become increasingly easy to do it," said Laura Seaman, principal scientist at Draper, during the livestream. "It's important to understand how these tools are being used and to identify them in an unknown situation."**

**When Iarpa launched the Felix program (short for Finding Engineering-Linked Indicators) that produced these efforts, the agency had set the ambitious goal of developing technologies that would be 90 percent effective at detecting the presence of engineering. In that regard,**

**the Iarpa awardees have some improving to do. In a test Iarpa ran this spring and announced October 17, government scientists evaluated the technology on 100 samples of both engineered and natural organisms taken from a variety of places, including soil, mouse feces, and a cow's stomach. Among these were 73 samples of bio-engineered organisms, many of which were mixed with other organisms that weren't engineered. "We tried to make these batches representative of the real-world challenges that the biosecurity community faces every day," Markowitz says.**

**According to Markowitz, the Draper and Ginkgo teams correctly identified 70 percent as being bio engineered. Draper had no false positives, while Ginkgo had one—results stating that bioengineering was detected when it was actually not present. A bigger problem for both teams was the rate of false negatives, or failing to identify bioengineering when it was in fact present. For one thing, the platforms didn't perform well on samples that contained very subtle genetic modifications, such as a single A or T that got swapped. These types of modifications can be made with a relatively new technique called base editing, which makes single base-letter changes instead of cutting whole genes or chunks of genes, like classic Crispr editing does.**

**"The larger the genome of the organism is, the more training data we need to get a statistical model, and the**

**more you have to sift through in order to find the signatures of engineering," Markowitz says.**

**Making the technology more accurate will require a bigger, more diverse dataset—more reference genomes of the organisms all around us. "We should be sequencing everything that is around us and monitoring what is there," says Joshua Dunn, head of design at Ginkgo. "It will help us understand the baseline of what is normal, so that if we see any deviation from that we can zero in on the parts of the sample that are the most interesting."**

**(Iarpa did not release performance data for technologies developed by the program's four other participants: The Broad Institute of MIT and Harvard, Harvard University's Wyss Institute, Noblis, and Raytheon.).But even if the platforms' accuracy improves, it's hard to know whether they would be able to detect a completely new organism that scientists have never seen before. Richard Ebright, a molecular biologist at Rutgers University, is skeptical that any technology will be able to definitively identify a bio-engineered organism. "There is no technology—none—that comprehensively and reliably can distinguish between an engineered genome sequence and a natural genome sequence, and there never will be," he says. "There are too many ways to manipulate a genome without leaving signatures of manipulation."**

**This includes a technique developed more than a decade ago called seamless ligation of nucleic acids, or Slice, which uses bacterial enzymes to join DNA fragments.**

**Older methods, such as selective breeding or serial passage—repeatedly growing viruses or bacteria in new environments over time—also would be unlikely to leave signatures of engineering, he says.**

**And Gigi Gronvall, a senior scholar at the Johns Hopkins Bloomberg School of Public Health who focuses on biosecurity, says the genetic sequence of a new pathogen isn't the only factor to consider when determining whether a biothreat has been engineered. "If there was suspicion of deliberate misuse, attributing that to a particular actor is going to rest on lots of pieces of evidence," she says. Factors such as where a new pathogen emerges, who it initially infects, and how it spreads, need to be considered. "Being able to identify these signatures that indicate bioengineering is important, and I hope we continue to get better at it. But it's never going to be 100 percent of the picture," she says.**

**Not all engineered organisms are dangerous, of course. Companies are engineering bacteria, viruses, plants, animals, and human cells with benefits that might help treat diseases or create new foods. Markowitz says bioengineering detection could help these companies protect their intellectual property.**

**But governments will likely be the main users of the technology. Markowitz says Iarpa has already made the platforms available to other US government agencies. ("I can't speak to how these tools are being used currently, but I will say that for several months they have been in the**

**hands of a very large number of both domestic and international partners," he says.)**

**And he confirmed that early on in the Covid-19 pandemic, Iarpa used technology from the Felix program to determine that the SARS-CoV-2 virus was not bio engineered. The idea that SARS-CoV-2 was engineered in a lab has since been thoroughly discredited, but at the time some scientists had questioned whether a part of the virus called the furin cleavage site, which is responsible for its high infectivity, was evidence of engineering, because some of the virus's closest relatives don't have this feature.**

**Gronvall says the theory flourished in part because of scientists' limited knowledge of coronaviruses. It turns zero and it's become increasingly easy to do it," said Laura Seaman, principal scientist at Draper, during the livestream. "It's important to understand how these tools are being used and to identify them in an unknown situation."**

**When Iarpa launched the Felix program (short for Finding Engineering-Linked Indicators) that produced these efforts, the agency had set the ambitious goal of developing technologies that would be 90 percent effective at detecting the presence of engineering. In that regard, the Iarpa awardees have some improving to do.**

**In a test Iarpa ran this spring and announced October 17, government scientists evaluated the technology on 100**

**samples of both engineered and natural organisms taken from a variety of places, including soil, mouse feces, and a cow's stomach. Among these were 73 samples of bioengineered organisms, many of which were mixed with other organisms that weren't engineered. "We tried to make these batches representative of the real-world challenges that the biosecurity community faces every day," Markowitz says.**

**According to Markowitz, the Draper and Ginkgo teams correctly identified 70 percent as being bioengineered. Draper had no false positives, while Ginkgo had one—results stating that bioengineering was detected when it was actually not present. A bigger problem for both teams was the rate of false negatives, or failing to identify bioengineering when it was in fact present. For one thing, the platforms didn't perform well on samples that contained very subtle genetic modifications, such as a single A or T that got swapped. These types of modifications can be made with a relatively new technique called base editing, which makes single base-letter changes instead of cutting whole genes or chunks of genes, like classic Crispr editing does.**

**The platforms also had a harder time detecting evidence of engineering in samples from organisms with large genomes, according to Markowitz. "The larger the genome of the organism is, the more training data you**

need to get a statistical model, and the more you have to sift through in order to find the signatures of engineering," Markowitz says.

Making the technology more accurate will require a bigger, more diverse dataset—more reference genomes of the organisms all around us. "We should be sequencing everything that is around us and monitoring what is there," says Joshua Dunn, head of design at Ginkgo. "It will help us understand the baseline of what is normal, so that if we see any deviation from that we can zero in on the parts of the sample that are the most interesting."

(Iarpa did not release performance data for technologies developed by the program's four other participants: The Broad Institute of MIT and Harvard, Harvard University's Wyss Institute, Noblis, and Raytheon.)

But even if the platforms' accuracy improves, it's hard to know whether they would be able to detect a completely new organism that scientists have never seen before. Richard Ebright, a molecular biologist at Rutgers University, is skeptical that any technology will be able to definitively identify a bioengineered organism. "There is no technology—none—that comprehensively and reliably can distinguish between an engineered genome sequence and a natural genome sequence, and there never will be," he says. "There are too many ways to manipulate a genome without leaving signatures of manipulation."

This includes a technique developed more than a decade ago called seamless ligation of nucleic acids, or Slice,

**which uses bacterial enzymes to join DNA fragments. Older methods, such as selective breeding or serial passage—repeatedly growing viruses or bacteria in new environments over time—also would be unlikely to leave signatures of engineering, he says.**

**And Gigi Gronvall, a senior scholar at the Johns Hopkins Bloomberg School of Public Health who focuses on biosecurity, says the genetic sequence of a new pathogen isn't the only factor to consider when determining whether a biothreat has been engineered. "If there was suspicion of deliberate misuse, attributing that to a particular actor is going to rest on lots of pieces of evidence," she says. Factors such as where a new pathogen emerges, who it initially infects, and how it spreads, need to be considered. "Being able to identify these signatures that indicate bioengineering is important, and I hope we continue to get better at it. But it's never going to be 100 percent of the picture," she says.**

**Not all engineered organisms are dangerous, of course. Companies are engineering bacteria, viruses, plants, animals, and human cells with benefits that might help treat diseases or create new foods. Markowitz says bioengineering detection could help these companies protect their intellectual property.**

**But governments will likely be the main users of the technology. Markowitz says Iarpa has already made the platforms available to other US government agencies. ("I can't speak to how these tools are being used currently,**

**but I will say that for several months they have been in the hands of a very large number of both domestic and international partners," he says.)**

**And he confirmed that early on in the Covid-19 pandemic, Iarpa used technology from the Felix program to determine that the SARS-CoV-2 virus was not bioengineered. The idea that SARS-CoV-2 was engineered in a lab has since been thoroughly discredited, but at the time some scientists had questioned whether a part of the virus called the furin cleavage site, which is responsible for its high infectivity, was evidence of engineering, because some of the virus's closest relatives don't have this feature.**

**Gronvall says the theory flourished in part because of scientists' limited knowledge of coronaviruses. It turns out other coronaviruses have these sites as well. "It only seemed suspicious until we looked at more of the coronavirus family and realized that our n was just really low. We were only sampling a very tiny portion of what was out there," she says. "Now that our field of knowledge is greater, it's not so unusual anymore."**

**Ultimately, these testing platforms might not only detect future engineered biothreats, but help deter labs from creating them in the first place. "Any would-be bad actor, just by virtue of knowing that the tools to rapidly detect what they're trying to do are out there, might think twice," Markowitz says.**

**Genetic engineering involves combining biochemistry and molecular biology techniques that start with the isolation of the genetic materials, followed by molecular cloning. It ends when GMOs, the organisms possessing recombinant DNA, are created.**

**Briefly, genetic engineering involves:**

***1. Isolation of the genetic materials***

**The purpose of this process is to acquire genetic molecules from the organism of interest. Depending on the end-use, the genetic material can be DNA isolated from the organism of interest or ribonucleic acids (RNA) extracted from the tissues or cells of interest.**

**Isolated RNAs are reverse-transcribed to generate complementary DNA (cDNA) molecules. This strategy is useful when dealing with mRNAs of genes that need some form of post-transcriptional modifications for their expression.**

***Molecular cloning***

**This process involves cutting, assembling, amplifying, and introducing the recombinant DNA into the host organisms. It consists of the following steps:**

## *DNA fragmentation*

**This step serves to single out the region of interest by eliminating non-target DNA molecules from the target ones. Traditionally, DNA fragmentation uses restriction enzymes, also known as restriction endonucleases, to cut the DNA at specific sequences into fragments.**

**It may also involve using the polymerase chain reaction (PCR) technique to modify or edit the nucleotide sequences of the target region. PCR or the digested fragments are separated by gel electrophoresis and**

## *DNA ligation*

**In this step, the prepared DNA fragments join with a vector, a DNA molecule serving as a DNA-importing vehicle. The success of this step requires that both ends of the purified fragments possess sequences recognizable by the same restriction enzymes that cut in the multiple cloning site of the vector.**

**The enzyme DNA ligase catalyzes the joining of DNA fragments to the digested vector, creating the recombinant DNA.**

### *Transformation of recombinant DNA*

**This step introduces the constructed recombinant DNA into cells of the host organism, allowing it to be taken up and expressed. Transformation can occur using physical transformation approaches such as heat-shock transformation and electroporation or chemical transformation.**

### 3. *Multiplication of host cells and recombinant protein expression*

**Host cells possessing the recombinant DNA are selected based on the selectable marker gene contained in the vector.**

**After selection, the host organisms can be cultured under the selective condition to increase the number of cells containing the recombinant DNA. The induction of the recombinant DNA expression results in the recombinant proteins.**

### *Benefits of Genetic Engineering*

**Genetic engineering is a technology in molecular biology that uses recombinant DNA technology to manipulate genetic materials. The technology aims to construct customized proteins or modify the working of biological systems, which leads to the creation of genetically modified organisms (GMOs).**

**The application of genetic engineering has improved and developed new techniques and technologies that advance our understanding of biological phenomena and elevate our well-being.**

**However, there are a few concerns, such as ethical issues and the safety of genetically modified foods about the technology. Here we discuss the benefits of genetic engineering alongside its application with the problems and risks associated with it.**

**Genetic engineering technology has been a springboard for developing new techniques and technologies that bring about the advancement of science and improve human welfare. The following are some of the advantages of genetic engineering and examples of real-world applications:**

***1. Enhancement of existing laboratory techniques***

**Genetic engineering is not a stand-alone technology, but it has improved and enhanced existing laboratory techniques. DNA sequencing technology is one of the laboratory techniques that became more powerful when recombination DNA technology was incorporated into its workflow.[2]**

**For instance:**

### *Sanger sequencing*

**Sanger sequencing is a chain-termination DNA sequencing technique that uses dideoxynucleotides to terminate the synthesizing DNA chains. At the start of the reaction, oligonucleotides anneal to the complementary DNA sequences before the chain synthesis and termination occur.**

**The priming of oligonucleotides limits the sequencing of DNA fragments to only those with partially known DNA sequences. With molecular cloning, the ligation of the target DNA fragment to vectors at the site where the DNA sequences are known can overcome this limitation.By doing so, oligonucleotides can anneal to the complementary region in the vector, enabling the sequencing of the unknown DNA fragment joined to the vector.[2]**

## *Large-scale DNA sequencing*

**Large-scale DNA sequencing, also known as shotgun DNA sequencing, is a DNA sequencing technique that accommodates long DNA fragments.**

**For example, in the early phase of the Human Genome Project, DNA is randomly broken and cloned into a bacteriophage sequencing vector, M13. This results in a library of clones containing the recombinant DNA.The clones are randomly selected and sequenced until no new identical recombinant DNA appears. The repeated clones are pooled and hybridized in the library to mark and eliminate clones containing DNA fragments identical to those already sequenced. This way, only the clones processing different DNA fragments are sequenced, and the covered region can be expanded.[3]**

## *Comprehensive understanding of biological phenomena*

**Apart from enhancing existing laboratory techniques, GMOs such as bacterial cells expressing recombinant proteins and transgenic animals have given scientists the tools to dissect, analyze, and describe several biological phenomena. These phenomena include the underlying cause of genetic diseases and disease pathology.**

## For example:

### *Gaucher Disease*

Gaucher disease (GD) is an inherited genetic disorder most prevalent in the Ashkenazi Jewish population. In GD patients, glucocerebroside, a type of glycolipids in the lysosome, is excessively accumulated. This is because of deficiencies in glucocerebrosidase (EC 3.2.1.45), the enzyme that usually degrades it.

Molecular cloning and sequencing of the gene encoding glucocerebrosidase, the alleles, and the neighboring region have enabled researchers to understand the change in the enzyme activity and its relationship to clinical manifestations of the disease.[4]

### *Spike Proteins*

The spike proteins of severe acute respiratory syndrome and the Middle East respiratory syndrome coronaviruses (SARS-CoV and MERS-CoV, respectively) play a role in the virus entry into host cells. This knowledge stemmed from experiments that used recombinant proteins containing variations of the spike proteins and potential host targets.

**Biochemical and cell biology experiments using recombinant proteins revealed that spike proteins from SARS-CoV and MERS-CoV interact with specific host proteins and hijack their way into the host cells.**

**When a similar virus, severe acute respiratory syndrome coronavirus 2 (SARS-CoV2), emerged at the end of 2019, cloning, sequencing, and PCR site-directed mutagenesis of the gene encoding its spike protein could identify the beneficial mutation that became fixed in the genome of the new virus. SARS-CoV2 recombinant spike protein expression illustrated its structure, host target, and viral cell entry mechanism, providing insights into potential vaccination targets and treatment strategies.(REF.*)**

***Neurodegenerative diseases such* as**

**Alzheime Neurodegenerative Diseasesr's disease, Parkinson's dementia, and Pick's disease are associated with an accumulation of microtubule-associated protein tau in the mammalian nervous system.**

**The nature of their manifestations has made the disease's mechanisms and tau dysfunctionality challenging to study. In this case, genetic engineering**

**provides the answer to the challenge in the creation of transgenic animals.**

**Caenorhabditis elegans, Drosophila melanogaster, Xenopus oocytes, and mice have been genetically manipulated to express various levels and forms of tau.**

**Studies of changes in the nervous system, tau dynamics, and neurological disease development in these genetically modified (GM) animals improve the understanding of neurodegenerative diseases and bring us closer to early diagnostic approaches and therapeutic intervention.[10]**

***Development of new t*echnologies**

**Not only can genetic engineering provide a better understanding of how biological systems work and respond, but it can also be a tool when the knowledge is used to create new technologies.**

**Fluorescent protein technology is an example of a new technology built by genetic engineering. It started by discovering the green and red fluorescent proteins (GFP and RFP, respectively) in jellyfish and sea corals.**

**When exposed to the lights of a suitable wavelength, RFP and GFP are chromophores that emit fluorescence without**

**any additional enzyme or co factor. Cloning and sequencing of the genes encoding GFP and RFP provide information on the three-dimensional structure of the proteins, unveiling the formation of chromophores and the emission of fluorescence.The findings permit scientists to use genetic engineering to manipulate the genes, hence creating the enhanced version of the proteins and changing the color of the chromophores. To date, the color palette of existing fluorescent proteins ranges in the blue-cyan, cyan-green, green, yellow, orange, red, and far-red spectra.**

**The same information also provided the basis for developing bimolecular fluorescence complementation (BiFC) assay, enabling scientists to confirm a protein-protein interaction and where the interaction occurs in living cells.**

### *Creation of new therapeutic approaches*

**Genetic engineering can use insights into the cause of a disease, its pathology, and its development to create new therapeutic approaches. Examples of these are:**

#### *Therapeutic Proteins*

**Therapeutic proteins are proteins used in replacement therapy to treat genetic disorders or certain medical conditions. Therapeutic proteins can**

**be extracted from human or animal cells, semi-synthesized, or genetically engineered in host cells in the laboratory. Examples of therapeutic recombinant proteins are human growth hormone and glucocerebrosidase used in replacement therapy for dwarfism and Gaucher disease.**

## *Gene Therapy*

**Gene therapy refers to a therapeutic strategy that overrides the effect of a dysfunctional gene allele in patients. It does so by introducing the patient's somatic cells to the functional allele of the gene or to the nucleic acids that modify the function of the defective allele.**

**In ex vivo gene therapy, the functional allele is inserted into the patient's cells, and the transected cells are transplanted back into the patient. One method is to use a viral vector vehicle to carry the functional gene into the cell. Here, genetic engineering replaces the viral genes involved in viral replication, or the nonessential genes, with the target gene.**

***In doing so, the viral vector cannot be replicated using the host machinery, and the protein of the inserted allele is created. The Oxford-AstraZeneca, Sputnik V,***

***Johnson and Johnson, and Convidecia COVID-19 vaccines are based on this method. Instead of a functional gene allele, a region from the viral spike protein is inserted into the vector and later translated as a target for antibody induction.***

**Alternatively, in vivo gene therapy directly delivers the gene products such as mRNA or short-interfering RNA (siRNA) to the patient's cells. This method starts with constructing a recombinant DNA that contains the cDNA of interest in a vector of choice.**

**The recombinant DNA is subsequently transcribed in vitro by RNA polymerase, purified, modified, and packaged for injection into the patient.**

**The Pfizer-BioNTech, Moderna, and CureVac mRNA-based vaccines against SARS-CoV2 are developed based on this approach. Similar to the viral vector COVID-19 vaccines, a region of the spike protein is translated and used to elicit an immune response in the vaccinated person.**

***Creation of characteristics not found in nature***

**The manipulation of DNA from different species can combine desirable features in one transgenic organism.**

**GMOs can be engineered to display a combination of customized characteristics that are otherwise not producible by other means.**

**Notable examples of such GMOs or their products are:**

***Taliglucerase alfa***

**Taliglucerase alfa, marketed as Elelyso, is the first FDA-approved plant-based pharmaceutical drug. It is a recombinant human glucocerebrosidase intended for enzyme replacement therapy in Gaucher disease patients.**

**Carrot cells, which do not naturally possess glucocerebrosidase, were genetically manipulated to express the protein and signal peptides necessary for posttranslational modification.**

**The choice of a plant-based production system was based on the fact that most people afflicted with Gaucher disease follow a Kosher diet, which prohibits non-certified animals or animal by-products.**

***Golden Rice***

**Golden Rice is the first transgenic plant genetically engineered to contain the entire beta-carotene biosynthesis pathway. Beta-carotene is a vitamin A precursor naturally produced in the leaf but not in the edible endosperm.**

**Genes encoding phytoene synthase from daffodils, carotene desaturase 1 and 2 from the bacterium Erwiniauredovora were cloned and constructed, and transferred to be expressed in the rice endosperm.**

**As the name suggests, golden rice produces yellow grains that are high in beta-carotene. It is thought that when consumed, beta-carotene in the grains can supplement vitamin A in the consumers. Since its inception, golden rice has been used as a parental line for several rice breeding programs.**

## *Issues and Risks of Genetic Engineering*

**Despite the pros of genetic engineering technology, its use remains debatable decades after the conception of the technology. The concerns over the use of genetic engineering revolve around the following issues:**

**(i) Health safety in the consumption of food or products produced from GM crops, which are generally engineered to contain antibiotic or pesticide resistance genes.**

**(ii) Ecological and environmental concerns over the cultivation of GM crops, which are based on the possibility of horizontal gene transfer and loss of genetic diversity.**

**(iii) Ethical issues over the welfare of animals used as experimental models and used in breeding programs.**

**(iv) Controversies surrounding whether genetic engineering in humans interferes with the evolutionary selection process and whether it is a modern form of eugenics.**

**Genetic engineering uses recombinant DNA technology to create genetically modified organisms or GMOs. It is one of the most powerful technologies available in molecular biology. On the other hand, it's also one of the most controversial. Nevertheless, the benefits of genetic engineering are so much more than creating new GMOs.**

**Its application also improves existing techniques, unravels complex biological processes and brings about new technologies and novel approaches. When used within the bounds of ethical and safety concerns, it brings about the technological advancement that can improve the quality of life.**

**The respiratory syndrome (SARS-CoV) and middle east respiratory syndrome (MERS-CoV)) did not produce even 1% of the global harm already inflicted by COVID-19. There are also four other CoVs capable of infecting humans (HCoVs), which circulate continuously in the human population, but their phenotypes are generally mild, and these HCoVs received relatively little attention. These dramatic differences between infection with HCoVs, SARS-CoV, MERS-CoV, and SARS-CoV-2 raise many questions, such as: Why is COVID-19 transmitted so quickly? Is it due to some specific features of the viral structure? Are there some specific human (host) factors? Are there some environmental factors? The aim of this review is to collect and concisely summarize the possible and logical answers to these questions.**

**CORONA -19 Virus itself is non living. However, other theory supports it to be living virus [1].**

**According to late English and advanced twentieth century dictionaries virus is slimy liquid, poison. Virus or antigen is a harmful substance discharged by the trillions of living organisms in the blood. Trillions of living organisms**

**discharged excretion in the blood, excretion contains antibody harmful substances called as virus or antigen.**

**There are three foundational tools for GENOME EDITNG . They are (i) clustered regularly interspaced short palindromic repeats (CRISPR)- CRISPR-associated protein 9 (Cas9), (ii) transcription activator-like effector nucleases (TALENs), and (iii) zinc-finger nucleases (ZFNs) for genome editing. CRISPR-Cas9 is a simple and powerful gene-editing technique. It consists of a single-cell immune system that allows for insertion and deletion of DNA. Virtually anyone can buy a CRISPR-Cas9 kit. They are sold online for less than a hundred dollars. The plasmids that come with the kits are generally benign substances like yeast and various plants that pose a very small risk to kit users.**

***Genome editing falls into a category of research and technology that's known as "dual-use". This means, it has the potential both for beneficial advances and harmful misuses. Genome editing could be used, for example, to eradicate disease carrying mosquitoes. In medical science, it has been widely used in (i)CANCER (ii)BLOOD DISORDER (iii) BLINDNESS, (iv)AIDS (v)CYSTIC FIBROSIS (vi) MUSCULAR DISTROPHY***

***(vii)HUNTINGTON'S DISEASE and (viii) the CREATION OF GENETICALLY MODIFIED BEAUTIFUL BABY IN THE HUMAN BEING [2] . These may be considerd positive. On the other hand,"Genome Editing" is included in a section on weapons of mass destruction.***

**In December 2019, a pneumonia outbreak was reported in Wuhan, China. On 31 December 2019, the outbreak was traced to a novel strain of coronavirus, which was given the interim name 2019-nCoV by the World Health Organization (WHO), later renamed SARS-CoV-2 by the International Committee on Taxonomy of Viruses. Some researchers have suggested the Huanan Seafood Wholesale Market may not be the original source of viral transmission to humans.**

- **As of 11th September 2020, there have been 913,919 confirmed deaths and more than 5,041,126 confirmed cases in the coronavirus pneumonia pandemic. The Wuhan strain has been identified as a new strain of Betacoronavirus from group 2B with approximately 70% genetic similarity to the SARS-CoV [3]. The virus has a 96% similarity to a *bat coronavirus*, so it is widely suspected to originate from bats as well show the similarity with the present CORONA -19 virus. More than 90 percent**

**of the constrains available in the AIDS , EBOLA ,INFLUENZA and MALARIA viruses show the similarity with the present COVID-19 virus.**

**Coronaviruses were discovered in the early 1930s when an acute respiratory infection of domesticated chickens was shown to be caused by a virus now known as avian infectious bronchitis virus (IBV). The first human coronaviruses (HCoV) were discovered in 1965. Research with human volunteers at the Common Cold Unit near Salisbury, UK, showed that colds could be induced by nasal washings that did not contain rhinoviruses. More experiments where nasal swabs were inoculated onto cultures of the respiratory tract revealed the presence of enveloped viruses with the characteristic shape of coronaviruses as previously described for causing bronchitis. The term coronavirus (Latin: corona, crown) was named for these viruses reflecting their characteristic fringed (crowned) appearance in the electron microscope after negative staining. Coronaviruses range in size from 80–120 nm (1/10 size of E. coli). The size of SARS-CoV-2, the virus that causes COVID-19, is about 120 nm, or 0.12 µ in diameter. N95 (masks) protect down to 0.1 µ, with 95% efficiency, which is why such masks have this name .**

**Coronaviruses are now recognized in a range of animal species causing respiratory, gastrointestinal, nervous, and systemic diseases. Coronaviruses are positive-sense, single-stranded RNA viruses that mutate faster than any life-form because they lack proofreading mechanisms in replication . In contrast, DNA viruses and other life-forms have proofreading enzymes that check the genome in replication. The COVID-19 pandemic began as a collection of pneumonia cases in December 2019, in Wuhan, China. At first, the virus was identified as 2019-nCoV by the World Health Organization, WHO. Then, as it has been studied and examined more, WHO officially named the virus as SARS-CoV-2 or(REF.*) the cause of COVID-19 disease.**

**Coronaviruses are members of the family Coronaviridae. This subfamily consists of four genera, or categories: alphacoronavirus (α-CoV), betacoronavirus (β-CoV), gammacoronavirus (γ-CoV),**
**and deltacoronavirus (δ-CoV) on the basis of their shared genetic relationships and genomes. Among the categories, SARS-CoV-2 is a β-CoV. In the variety of the different coronaviruses, there have been six separate strains that are known to infect humans. In the six strains, four of them have low pathogenicity and cause mild symptoms.**

**Although the other two strains, SARS-CoV and MERS-CoV, are more severe and can be fatal. SARS-CoV-2 is among the severe strains of coronavirus, more specifically from the SARS-CoV strain. This has been tested and proven through comparing SARS-CoV-2 with the bat CoV and SARS-CoV. SARS-CoV-2 was 96% identical to bat CoV and 80% identical to SARS-CoV, the virus that caused SARS in 2003. The two highly pathogenic viruses, SARS-CoV and MERS-CoV, cause severe respiratory syndrome in humans, and the other four human coronaviruses induce only mild upper respiratory diseases (i.e. colds) in healthy people, although some of them can cause severe infections in infants, young children, and senior citizens.**

**According to the CDC (2020), individuals suffering with COVID-19 experience a wide range of symptoms ranging from mild to severe illness. COVID-19's symptoms are similar to influenza symptoms which include fever, cough, shortness of breath, and difficulty breathing. In severe cases, acute pneumonia, severe respiratory syndrome, renal insufficiency, and even death can occur . Symptoms may appear 2–14 days after exposure to the virus. In order to better understand the background and important factors of COVID-19, it is vital to look further into the**

**origin of it. Bat coronaviruses SARS-CoV and MERS-CoV, a type of bat coronavirus that passes through camels, were strains that appeared before the SARS-CoV-2 strain. In 2002 and 2003, there was an outbreak with SARS-CoV that killed 774 people before it was able to be controlled. Then, in 2012, there was an outbreak with MERS-CoV that killed 884 people. Despite those outbreaks happening, scientific research was more focused on significant viruses such as influenza. A few scientists tried to warn about a harmful potential re-emergence of the SARS-CoV, but those warnings were not heeded. Now that SARS-CoV-2 has been studied more since it has started a pandemic, researchers have learned more about its structure and mutations within the strain that have caused it to become the deadly virus scientists feared it would become. Scientists confirmed that SARS-CoV-2 uses the same human body cell entry receptor—angiotensin-converting enzyme II (ACE2)—as SARS-CoV-1. This would make it "natural" and not a bio-engineered virus. The reason that a human bio-engineered strain is unlikely is that the binding site for virus entry to a human body cell is not "ideal," that is, not as precise as one made in biotechnology. A man-made virus would be very efficient for binding to the human receptor. Additionally, the backbone of the virus does not resemble any previously**

**described in scientific literature used for genetic modification. Comparative analysis of genetic (RNA) data suggests SARS-CoV-2 may bind human hACE2, just like the first SARS outbreak in 2002. The computational analyses predict that this interaction is not ideal (random in nature) and therefore likely rules out laboratory manipulations as a potential origin for SARS-CoV-2 ( REF.*).**

**A prominent mutation on the surface of the SARS-CoV-2 increased its virulence. This mutation modified a glycoprotein spike on the virus surface which it uses to bind to and enter respiratory system cells. The mutation produced a cleavage site for the human protease called furin. Furin modified the spike glycoprotein on the surface of SARS-CoV-2 allowing it to more optimally bind and enter throat and lung cells. This made SARS-CoV-2 more deadly to vulnerable humans (REF.*). As the funds for research are increased drastically for this virus, knowing the specific mutations within the SARS-CoV-2 strain is helpful to scientists trying to find a vaccine and treatment. Even though past research was not taken as seriously as it perhaps should have been for SARS-CoV, the current research being conducted will hopefully combat the spread of COVID-19. Severe acute respiratory syndrome**

**coronavirus (SARS-CoV) and Middle East respiratory syndrome coronavirus (MERS-CoV) are two highly transmissible and pathogenic viruses that emerged in humans at the beginning of the 21st century. Genetically diverse coronaviruses that are related to SARS-CoV and MERS-CoV were discovered in bats worldwide (REF.*). This diversity and potential spillover of bat-borne coronaviruses are evidenced by the origin and genesis of pathogenic coronaviruses. In one of the earliest studies to examine the "genesis" or origin of the Wuhan coronavirus, Professor Pei Hao at the Pasteur Shanghai Institute performed genetic analysis on the collection of coronavirus sequences from various animals and humans. His data indicated that SARS-CoV-2 belongs to the betacoronavirus genera and shares a common ancestor with the SARS/SARS-like coronaviruses (including those causing the SARS epidemic). Their common ancestor resembles the bat coronavirus strain similar to SARS (2003), yet distinct (RaTG13 is a unique RNA sequence in SARS-CoV-2). Based on the genetic relationship of betacoronavirus, the bat is likely the native host of the SARS-CoV-2. Previous studies showed that CoV's genomes display a high degree of change (plasticity) in terms of RNA and recombination. Furthermore, the relatively large CoV genome increases the probabilities for**

**adaptive mutations, with it being relatively easy for the spike protein to exploit multiple body cell receptors for virus attachment and entry (REF.*).**

## The Wild Side of Life: Displacement and How Sylvatic Diseases Become Urban Diseases

## Zoonotic Spillover Cycle—Spillover from Bats to People

> **Its original structure and or function was made good in its original place or position; however in a new position or place, due to the curse of Genesis 3, it is now functioning poorly or pathogenically.**

**Zoonosis is an infectious disease caused by a pathogen that has jumped from non-human animals (usually vertebrates) to humans. Animals can sometimes carry microbes, some "good" and some pathogenic that can spread to people and cause illness. The sylvatic cycle, also known as the "wild" transmission cycle, is a portion of the natural transmission cycle of a pathogen or parasite. Sylvatic refers to the occurrence of a subject in or affecting wild animals. The sylvatic cycle is the fraction of the pathogen population's lifespan spent cycling between wild animals and vectors.**

**Humans are usually an incidental or dead-end host, infected by a vector (REF.*).**

**In creation microbiology, displacement is the moving of something from its original designed place or purposeful position. Its original structure and or function was made good in its original place or position; however in a new position or place, due to the curse of Genesis 3, it is now functioning poorly or pathogenically. Microbes, including viruses, were originally designed for restricted places and good functions, but after the fall they spread to other places and began to cause disruption and disease. Sometimes, mutations in RNA, DNA, or proteins cause disease. In other cases, existing genetic information gets lost, duplicated, transferred, or changed. Modification of genetic information in a microbe kind and displacement thus probably led to its pathogenicity. Displacement can also be considered a horizontal transfer of genes, pathogens, and parasites to a different location in nature, often where the sylvatic cycle intersects the urban cycle (REF.*).**

**This specific strain of the virus was first reported to have originated in Wuhan, China, in a small fish market called the Huanan Seafood Market (REF.*). It was noted that**

**this wet market sold more than its name suggested, and in addition to the traditional seafood that was offered there, animals ranging from snakes and porcupines to beavers and bats could be found. Wet markets are not uncommon in China and are considered to be a part of their culture. In fact, public health experts note that Chinese culture is very fond of eating fresh foods, including meats and wild game. This practice introduces a new opportunity for zoonotic diseases and infections to be introduced to the human population (Rothan & Byrareddy 2020). Zoonotic diseases, diseases that pass from an animal to a human, make up approximately 70% (over 200 known diseases) of the diseases we see infecting populations today. The events in which the zoonotic diseases are spread from animals to humans are known as a zoonotic spillover. Zoonotic spillovers occur when an intermediate host, such as a bat with a high pathogenic count, comes in contact with a definitive host, a human, and the pathogen is transmitted from the reservoir population into the host population. In addition to the similarity in genetics to the horseshoe bat , the coronavirus strains have some similarities (phylogenetically) to SARS-CoV-2 in pangolins (scaly anteaters) that are found in Southeast Asia . Even though bat and pangolin viruses are closely related to SARS-CoV-2, none of the existing SARS-CoVs represent an immediate**

**direct ancestor. The RNA sequence from an intermediate horseshoe bat in Yunnan is closest to the genomic region of SARS-CoV-2. The host receptor domains (RBD) are closest to pangolins in Guangzhou China (REF.*). RBDs are sections of protein that directly engage with the receptors of viruses. Viral recombination occurs when viruses of two different parent strains coinfect the same host cell during replication to generate virus-containing genes from both parents (REF.*). The pangolin virus probably interacted with the human SARS-CoV-2 or was transmitted directly from the bat. Potential recombination sites suggest SARS-CoV-2 might be a recombinant virus, with its genome (RNA) backbone originated from the Yunnan bat virus-like SARS-related-CoVs and its RBD region acquired from the pangolin virus-like SARS-related-CoVs. Which came first is difficult to determine; however, it is fairly clear that the viruses have mixed RNA. A comparison of five key amino acids isolated from spike proteins of viruses in humans, pangolins, and horseshoe bats. Lines reveal probable virus variation and ancestry due to mutation.**

**There are current theories that scientists are working through to identify and trace back this new mutation of the coronavirus to determine what creature could be**

**responsible for this groundbreaking pandemic. The role of wild animals in human infections, including that resulting from the Wuhan breakout, should never be downplayed. Wet markets for example, though a current cultural component in Chinese countries, can introduce infections and diseases and should be re-evaluated with new laws to prevent future problems.**

## *Mysterious Origin of COVID-19:*

> **How did this lethal coronavirus jump from the wild in China to major human population centers?**

**The best scientists all over the world are working to understand SARS-CoV-2 and COVID-19 but there remains a mystery. How did this lethal corona virus jump from the wild in China to major human population centers? And what genetic mutations produced a pathogen that is so perfectly adapted to infect so many? Approximately 70% of emerging infectious diseases in humans are zoonotic, i.e., transmitted from an animal to a person. Genetic sequencing revealed SARS-CoV-2 is related to two other coronaviruses that originated in bats.**

**Its presumed SARS-CoV-2 originated in bats, though an intermediate host has yet to be identified.**

**The immediate source of SARS-CoV-2 remains a mystery even though the Wuhan market was initially suspected to be the epicenter of the epidemic. However, the closely related SARS-CoV-2 strains suggest the Wuhan outbreak probably originated from a point source with subsequent human-to-human transmission, in contrast to the multiple (polyphyletic) origin of MERS coronavirus. If the Wuhan market was the source, it is possible that bats carrying the parental (the bat coronavirus) virus were mixed in the market, enabling viral recombination. However, none of the animal samples from the market were reported to be positive, and the first identified case-patient and other early case-patients had not visited the market, suggesting the possibility of an alternative source (REF.*).**

## *Bat Viruses Displaced*

**Early investigations about the origin of COVID-19 suggested that the SARS-CoV-2 may have jumped from bats to humans. This is not unprecedented since bat viruses have been shown to "jump" the species barrier frequently to infect new species. However, since bats were**

**in hibernation when the outbreak occurred, and it was uncertain whether bats were sold at the market, the virus is more likely to have been transmitted via other species on the market. Genomic analyses of SARS-CoV-2 demonstrate a 96% nucleotide identity with a CoV isolated from a bat. Previous reports showed that species from the bat genera Rhinolophus in southern China contain a rich pool of SARS-like-CoVs. Interestingly, Chinese researchers showed that pangolin CoV sequences with 86% to 92% similarity to SARS-CoV-2. Early preliminary studies show the existence of lineages of pangolin CoVs with genetic similarity to SARS-CoV-2. Later the hypothesis that pangolins served as a potential intermediate host was not supported. The currently available data do not fully elucidate if the virus was directly transmitted from bats to humans or indirectly through an intermediate host. Consequentially, more sequence data is needed to confirm the specific source and origin of the SARS-CoV-2, which can only be achieved by enhanced collection and monitoring of bat and other wild animal samples. Furthermore, results are similar to the finding from other preliminary reports that indicate that the virus source of interspecies transmission was highly concentrated or limited, possibly a single event. In addition, the high sequence similarity among the viruses**

**isolated from patients indicates a recent introduction to humans. A study of cultured bat cells shows that their strong immune responses can drive viruses to greater virulence. Modeling bat immune systems on a computer, the researchers showed that when bat cells quickly release interferon upon infection, other cells quickly wall themselves off. This drives viruses to faster reproduction. The increased virulence and infectivity wreak havoc when these viruses infect animals with "tamer" immune systems, like humans.**

> ***Bats are hosts to 100 different viruses, many of which are harmful or potentially lethal to humans.***

**Bats have distinct characteristics that make them unique to most mammals. Perhaps their most recognizable feature is that bats are the only mammals that can truly fly. However, bats are hosts to 100 different viruses, many of which are harmful or potentially lethal to humans. An international research team led by Dr. Peng Zhou performed extensive bat studies. Their research aimed to discover how bats carry so many of these viruses without harm. They found that bats "turn on" an immune response that fights off danger. Mammals including**

**humans have this ability where they are able to regulate their immune response by "turning on" or "switching off" the response when danger is or is not present. This on/off switch is essential for protection and fighting off threats; however, it can be harmful and pose risks to the animal in certain instances. In other mammals, having the immune response constantly switched on is dangerous: it is pathogenic to tissue and cells. Bats never seem to turn off their immune system even when there are no threats, and yet this operates in harmony with their bodies. This allows the bat to carry 100 viruses without getting sick and to easily transmit these viruses to other mammals and humans (REF.*). Since bats were in hibernation in Wuhan when the epidemic started, this may not hold well for the Wuhan Institute of Virology (WIV). As the WHO investigates, it is doubtful they will find direct evidence that SARS-CoV-2 originated in the lab. The bat viruses in the lab were collected in Yunan province, hundreds of miles away from Wuhan. However, studying the distribution and emergence of bat coronaviruses in Yunan and Wuhan may provide circumstantial evidence. If SARS-CoV-2 is more similar to bat coronaviruses in Yunan than in Wuhan, it is possible that it originated in the lab from their studying bat viruses sampled elsewhere. In 2004, there were lab infections of SARS-CoV in Beijing**

**and in Singapore. The WIV found the origin of SARS-CoV in bats and are publishing sequences as they become available. Most interestingly, the sequence of the RaTG13 strain of bat virus, which is 96% similar to SARS-CoV-2, was isolated and published together with SARS-CoV-2. There is a possibility that the Wuhan Virology Lab had collected a natural sample from a market or bat source in Yunnan to study, and somehow the virus escaped the lab. This type of accidental escape has happened before with SARS-CoV (REF.*).**

**A highly pathogenic and severe disease, COVID-19, has been caused by SARS-CoV-2, Severe Acute Respiratory Syndrome Coronavirus 2. COVID-19 likely began in Wuhan, China, and has spread across the world. There are multiple coronaviruses, but the most harmful strains are SARS-CoV and MERS-CoV. SARS-CoV-2 shares a distant common ancestor to the SARS-CoV bat strain but has undergone different genetic mutations within its structure to make it more dangerous and even deadly to humans. The transmission of the disease has been found to be human-to-human contact while the origin is still somewhat of a mystery regarding its exact origin .**

**Viruses are news makers. They usually get bad press. But not all viruses are harmful. A virus needs a host and invades all types of hosts: bacteria, plants, animals, and humans. Viruses are supporting life on earth via recycling and controlling populations of microbes, plants, and some animals. They control many deadly animal pathogens and cancers in both animals and humans. They also protect human and animal intestinal (gut) functioning. They indirectly may help with digestion and absorption of food, protect against cancers, and stimulate the immune system.**

**Although research is still ongoing, viruses may protect and enhance the bat microbiome. Coronaviruses do not harm bats. There is strong evidence that viruses in mammals' (including bats) guts may protect our good microflora from the mammalian immune system (REF.*).**

**A scalpel or sharp instrument in the hand of a skilled surgeon or biologist is useful; the same sharp instrument in the hands of a thief or murderer will cause havoc. Regulation, control, and placement of a dangerous instrument are needed—so too in viruses. Viruses, even though small and simpler than most cells, possess tremendous designs. Creation microbiologists believe viruses were created for good uses in creation, but some**

**viruses were altered after the fall. Viruses are harmful when in places they should not be. This is referred to as displacement theory in creation biology. In the human genome, for instance, we have more DNA or RNA base sequences that align with viruses than we have bases that code for our own proteins. Some of these virus sequences (transpositions) in the human body make proteins that turn our immune system on and off, for example during pregnancy. Could some viruses then originate from animals and from us? If so, this supports the displacement creation theory, and, as we have stated above, many infectious viruses in humans have a zoonotic origin. For instance, we have heard about the swine and the bird flues. In these cases, human and bird influenza (flu) viruses mix in pigs, and new influenza viruses re-assort from mixture of the viral parts. These types of new influenza strains are usually the most virulent, infectious, and pathogenic (REF.*). In pandemics, new viruses that often emerge are a mixture of the viral sequences from various animals.**

> **Historically, evolutionists have told us that changes in living things happen at a slow and deliberate pace. Yet the creation model shows**

**that life is able to adapt to new environments rapidly.**

**Historically, evolutionists have told us that changes in living things happen at a slow and deliberate pace. Yet the creation model shows that life is able to adapt to new environments rapidly. Viral mechanisms of change include mutation and variation. RNA viruses, like SARS-CoV-2, are characterized by a high mutation rate and replicate up to a million times faster than their host. This mutation rate drives genome variability and enables the virus to escape the host's immunity (REF.*). Genetic variation explains differences in immune response strengths which may affect the susceptibility and the severity of infection of SARS-CoV-2 (REF.*).**

**Coronavirus genomes have genomic "flexible" genomes due to having high mutation rates and high rates of RNA recombination. Even on June 14, 2020, the strain identified in the Beijing COVID-19 outbreak is not like the type circulating in China according to the CDC chief epidemiologist.3 We see a displacement with modification that occurs when wild animals, like bats, transmit viruses to other species, like humans. This is commonly seen in wilderness, jungle, or desert environments. In the example**

**of the bat, the bat is unharmed because their immune system is able to fight off the threat. However, when the virus is transmitted to humans, our immune system is unable to fight it off. Mixing of genetic information occurs and new strains, species, and diseases arise. This is why not all diseases are created equally and old diseases take new forms. We now have a new disease that we need to trust God as our Shelter, Refuge, and Fortress (REF.*).**

**The Genesis of Germs (REF.*) provides some understanding of the origin of such diseases. From a biblical worldview, we can say that infectious diseases and pathogenesis became a secondary condition, a result of sin against our Creator. The sequence of events in a biblical worldview might be seen as Creation, Curse, Corruption, Contagion, and Crisis. In time, we will see what happens with the new Coronavirus Crisis and the signature "plague" of the new millennium.**

## *ReferencesAB*

****Andersen, Kristian G., Andrew Rambaut, W. Ian Lipkin, Edward C. Holmes & Robert F. Garry. "The proximal origin of SARS-CoV-2." Nature Medicine 26 (2020): 450–452.**

**Centers for Disease Control and Prevention. "Frequently Asked Questions." Coronavirus Disease 2019 (COVID-19) 2020. https://www.cdc.gov/coronavirus/2019-ncov/faq.html.

**Cui, J., Fang Li & Zheng-Li Shi." Origin and evolution of pathogenic coronaviruses." Nature Reviews, Microbiology 17, no. 3 (2019): 181–192. https://doi.org/10.1038/s41579-018-0118-9.

**Francis, Joe. "COVID-19, Coronavirus, and Creation Virology." (March 21, 2020). https://answersingenesis.org/coronavirus/covid19-coronavirus-and-creation-virology/and the Coming Plagues in a Fallen World. Green Forest, Arkansas: Master Books, 2019.

**Gillen, Alan L. and Keoprommony Huy. "Wise Blood: The Principle of Overcoming in Disease and Immunity (Part 1)." Answers in Depth 15 (Jan. 28,2020).

https://answersingenesis.org/human-b

## *SUMMARY:*

*Majority of scientists established the result that COVID-19 from the Genome sequence analysis is a natural virus and very few scientists found from experimental result of COVID-19 virus as a laboratory derived from the culture of corona virus, which appeared in 2002-2003 in 28 different countries and killed about 800 persons. But the present COVID-19 virus which appeared in December 2019 in China had great transmissibility and infectivity rate compared to 2002-2003 corona virus. This can not be created from the culture of virus, as it can give mutation of virus only and infectivity and transmissibility rate can not achieved in a tremendous way. For this we propose the theory of origin of COVID-19 virus. In* **this theory,** the *Genome Editing tool (CRISPR-Cas9) has been used to the novel CORONAVIRUS (nCoV) ,which appeared in 2002-2003 in GUANDONG Province of CHINA with the inclusion of some of the constrains of INFLUENZA, MALARIA, EBOLA and AIDS viruses by the scientists of the Microbiology Research institute using the Biological Scissor. This type of Genome editing and inclusion of FOUR Viruses ( some of the constrains of INFLUENZA, MALARIA,EBOLA and AIDS, respectively) in the novel CORONOVIRUS is possible in Microbiological Laboratory only, as the scientists are doing research work in CONONOVIRUS since 2000 beginning itself and they are* *expert in this field and have the technical and scientific know how sufficiently in this type of research problem. COVID-19 contains an uncommon genetic sequence that has been used by genetic engineers in the past to insert genes into coronaviruses( 26 to 32 kilobases) without leaving a trace, and it falls at the exact point that would allow experimenters to swap out different genetic parts to change the infectivity and transmissibility . That same sequence can occur naturally in a coronavirus. The Genome Editing tool (CRISPR-Cas9) has been used to the novel CORONAVIRUS (nCoV) ,which appeared in 2002-2003 in GUANDONG Province of CHINA with the inclusion of some of the constrains of INFLUENZA,MALARIA, EBOLA and AIDS viruses to increase the infectivity and transmissibility in a tremendous manner to spread throughout the world .*

**In addition to this, there are other several unique features that point out the fact that SARS-CoV-2 coronavirus was a MAN MADE VIRUS, rather than emerging through natural spillover from animals. They are as follows:**

**(i) CORONA-19 Viruses are considered to be non- living** *(REF.1A)***due to the characteristics like (a)They lack metabolic activity outside the living cells.(b)They lack cellular organisation. Once they infect a cell they take over the machinery of the host cell to replicate themselves.(c)They lack ribosomes and cellular enzymes**

**necessary for nucleic acid and protein synthesis. (d) They don't show cell division, growth, development ,nutrition etc.(e) They can be crystallized .(f) They don't contain both RNA and DNA together.**

**(ii)The presence of the spike glycoprotein and a novel lineage B betacoronavirus (βCoV), has caused a global pandemic of coronavirus disease (COVID-19).(Ref2A)**

**(iii) It has been speculated that RRAR, a unique furin-like cleavage site (FCS) in the spike protein (S), and it is absent in other lineage B βCoVs, such as SARS-CoV, is responsible for its high infectivity and transmissibility..(Ref 3A)**

**(iv) The report given by Dr. Li-Meng Yan of HongKong Public Health Department states that SARS-CoV-2 is "suspiciously" similar to two strains of bat coronaviruses, called ZC45 and ZXC21, that were discovered by scientists at military labs in China. [Ref.4A]The authors claim these strains could have been used as a template to clone a deadlier virus. But other scientists do not support this idea.**

**(v) phylogenetic analysis of SARS-CoV-2 identified an insertion of RRAR (FCS) at the S1/S2 site of SARS-CoV-2-S,[REF5A] which is absent in SARS-CoV and other SARS-related coronaviruses (SARSr-CoVs), family. It is the seventh known coronavirus to infect humans; four of these coronaviruses (229E, NL63, particularly RaTG13, which has 96% identity of its genomic sequence to that of SARS-CoV-2[Ref 4A] The COVID-19 is acute respiratory syndrome coronavirus 2 (SARS-CoV-2), which belongs to the β coronavirus OC43, and HKU1) only cause slight symptoms of the common cold. Conversely, the other three, SARS-CoV, MERS-CoV, and SARS-CoV-2, are able to cause severe symptoms and even death, with fatality rates of 10%, 37%, and 5%, respectively. The inclusion of strains of EBOLA, INFLUENZA, MALARIA, AIDS viruses in the CORONAVIRUS (nCoV) has increased its transmissibility and infectivity in a tremendous way to spread COVID -19 throughout the world and killing more than 8 million people ( official data), but the actual data is about 20 million death.**

**(vi) The SARS-CoV-2 has "restriction-enzyme sites," or genetic sequences that can be cut and manipulated by enzymes.[Ref6A] These genomic features are sometimes used in cloning, and the report claims their presence is indicative of an engineered virus. But scientists point out**

**these sites naturally occur in all types of genomes, from bacteria to humans.**

***The focus on the origin of the cell is not restricted to the study of energy-generating organelles. Indeed, scientists spend much time and debate on the fundamental question of how gradients of protons separated by cell membranes responsible for the energy creation in primordial conditions. In addition, studies of cell origin focus on the evolution of multicellularity, the state of cells cooperating to form a single organism, a large step toward the creation of the vertebrates and invertebrates we know today. Comparative genomics has helped map out these paths to multicellularity and diagram evolutionary divergence as well as Scientists study the structure and function of mitochondria and chloroplasts as well as their fascinating separate genomes to see what evidence might be left of the entities they once were. The focus on the origin of the cell is not restricted to the study of energy-generating organelles. Indeed, scientists spend much time and debate on the fundamental question of how gradients of protons separated by cell membranes enabled energy creation in primordial conditions. In addition, studies of cell origin focus on the evolution of***

***multicellularity*, the state of cells cooperating to form a single organism, a large step toward the creation of the vertebrates and invertebrates we know today. Comparative genomics has helped map out these paths to multicellularity and diagram evolutionary divergence as well as convergence.**

***The following criteria was given for identification of different viruses , which involved giving equal weight to the importance of type of nucleic acid (DNA or RNA);virion size( determined by ultrafiltration and electron microscopy);virion morphologya( determined by electron microscopy);virion stability (  determined by varying pH and temperature, exposure to lipid solvents and detergents),.; and virion antigenicity ( determined by various serological methods).***

## ***CORONA-19 VIRUS BRIEF DISCRIPTION:***

***Virus is the microorganisms which have the properties of living and non-living both. They have a specific structure which consists of  head and tail. Head is composed of several protein units known as capsomeres which enclose the genetic material made  up of  RNA or DNA. They have a lipid envelope derived from the host cell membrane which lies outside the capsomere. They occur in***

*crystalline form outside the body of the host but as it enters the host cell ,it injects its genetic material which replicates vigorously. The replicated materials are further packed in the new protein coat formed using host protein and is thrown out by the destruction of cell membrane.*

*CORONA -19 Virus itself is non living. However, other theory supports it to be living virus [1].*

*According to late English and advanced twentieth century dictionaries virus is slimy liquid, poison. Virus or antigen is a harmful substance discharged by the trillions of living organisms in the blood. Trillions of living organisms discharged excretion in the blood, excretion contains antibody harmful substances called as virus or antigen.*

*There are three foundational tools for GENOME EDITNG . They are (i) clustered regularly interspaced short palindromic repeats (CRISPR)- CRISPR-associated protein 9 (Cas9), (ii) transcription activator-like effector nucleases (TALENs), and (iii) zinc-finger nucleases (ZFNs) for genome editing. CRISPR-Cas9 is a simple and powerful gene-editing technique. It consists of a single-cell immune system that allows for insertion and deletion of DNA. Virtually anyone can buy a CRISPR-Cas9 kit. They are sold online for less* **than a hundred dollars. The plasmids that come with the kits are generally benign substances like yeast and various plants that pose a very small risk to kit users.**

***Genome editing falls into a category of research and technology that's known as "dual-use". This means, it has the potential both for beneficial advances and harmful misuses. Genome editing could be used, for example, to eradicate disease carrying mosquitoes. In medical science, it has been widely used in (i)CANCER (ii)BLOOD DISORDER (iii) BLINDNESS, (iv)AIDS (v)CYSTIC FIBROSIS (vi) MUSCULAR DISTROPHY (vii)HUNTINGTON'S DISEASE and (viii) the CREATION OF GENETICALLY MODIFIED BEAUTIFUL BABY IN THE HUMAN BEING [2] . These may be considerd positive. On the other hand,"Genome Editing" is included in a section on weapons of mass destruction.***

**As of 11th September 2020, there have been 913,919 confirmed deaths and more than 5,041,126 confirmed cases in the coronavirus pneumonia pandemic. The Wuhan strain has been identified as a new strain of Betacoronavirus from group 2B with**

**approximately 70% genetic similarity to the SARS-CoV [3]. The virus has a 96% similarity to a *bat coronavirus*, so it is widely suspected to originate from bats as well show the similarity with the present CORONA -19 virus. More than 90 percent of the constrains available in the AIDS , EBOLA ,INFLUENZA and MALARIA viruses show the similarity with the present COVID-19 virus.**

***SARS was determined to be contained in mid-2003 by the WHO, with a total of 8,098 cases and 774 deaths in 26 different countries. MERS is not yet contained but is attributed to just under 2,500 cases and 858 deaths in 27 countries.***

***French Nobel prize winning scientist Luc Montagnier has made the claim that the SARS-CoV-2 virus came from a lab, and is the result of an attempt to manufacture a vaccine against the AIDS virus [11] . Professor Montagnier was awarded the 2008 Nobel Prize in Medicine for the identification of AIDS virus, with his colleague professor Françoise Barre-Sinoussi.***

## *CONCLUSION*

The COROA -19 is a non-living virus prepared in the Microbiology Laboratory under very high secret

BIOLOGICAL WAR weapon Programme and not originated from the bat as natural living virus , as mostly claimed by the scientists of China or other countries.

**CORONA-19 (SARS-CoV-2) is made using the biological scissors of CRISPR-CaS9 genome editing tool by the inclusion of some strains of EBOLA, INFLUENZA, MALARIA and AIDS viruses in the CORONA VIRUS (nCoV) and in this way it has increased its transmissibility and infectivity in a tremendous way to spread the disease COVID -19 throughout the world.**

***REFERENCES:***

*REF 1A:Viruses—Living or Non-Living?*

*ROSS AIKEN GORTNER*

*SCIENCE*

*10 Jun 1938*

*Vol 87, Issue 2267*

*pp. 529-530*

*DOI: 10.1126/science.87.2267.529*

- ***Open Access***
- ***Published: 12 REF 2ALetter***
- ***June 2020***

## *REF. 2A: The role of furin cleavage site in SARS-CoV-2 spike protein-mediated membrane fusion in the presence or absence of trypsin*


- ***Shuai Xia, Qiaoshuai Lan, Shan Su,***
- ***Xinling Wang, Wei Xu, Zezhong Liu,***
- ***Yun Zhu, Qian Wang, Lu Lu & Shibo Jiang***


***Signal Transduction and Targeted Therapy volume 5, Article number: 92 (2020)***

- ***REF 3A ;DOI:10.1101/2020.08.25.266775***
- 
- ***Corpus ID: 221355647***


***The S1/S2 boundary of SARS-CoV-2 spike protein modulates cell entry pathways and transmission***


- ***Yunkai Zhu, Fei Feng, +15 authors Rong Zhang***



- ***Published 25 August 2020***
- ***Biology***
- ***bioRxiv***


***The global spread of SARS-CoV-2 is posing major public h***

***Mol Biol Evol. 2022 Jan; 39(1): msab327.***

***Published online 2021 Nov 12. doi: 10.1093/molbev/msab327***

***REF.5A :PMCID: PMC8689951***
***PMID: 34788836***

***The Emergence of the Spike Furin Cleavage Site in SARS-CoV-2***

***Yujia Alina Chan1 and Shing Hei Zhan2***

***REF.4A:The Wuhan Laboratory Origin of SARS-CoV-2 and the Validity of the Yan Reports Are Further Proved by the Failure of Two Uninvited "Peer Reviews" Opening Statement***

- ***March 2021***

***DOI:10.5281/zenodo.4650821***

- ***REF.4A: Project: COVID-19***

***Authors:***

***Limeng Yan***

- ***The University of Hong Kong***

***Shu Kang***
***Shanchang Hu***
***Preprints and early-stage research may not have been peer reviewed yet***

***REF.: 5A: Engineering SARS-CoV-2 using a reverse genetic systemXuping Xie, Kumari G. Lokugamage, Xianwen***

*Zhang, Michelle N. Vu, Antonio E. Muruato, Vineet D. Menachery andPei-Yong Shi*

*Nature Protocols volume 16, pages1761–1784 (2021)Cite this article*

***REF. 6A Endonuclease fingerprint indicates a synthetic origin of SARS-CoV-2***

***View ORCID ProfileValentin Bruttel, View ORCID ProfileAlex Washburne, View ORCID ProfileAntonius VanDongen***
***doi: https://doi.org/10.1101/2022.10.18.512756***

***RoberT. Preidt (2020): Health News , March 26, 2020.***

***2 Antonio Regalado(2018). Exclusive:Chinese Scientists are creating CRISPR babes :NATURE:BIOTECHNOLOGY:CRISPR.***

***3. Hsin-Chou Yang,Chun-houh Chen,Jen Hung Wang,Hsiao-Chi Liao,Chih-Ting Chun-How Kao,Mei-Yeh Jade Lu and James C. Liao Analysis***

*uence analysis of SARS-CoV-2 genome reveals features important for vaccine design , NATURE :Scientific Reports 10, No. 15643, Sept 24, 2020.of geonomic distributions of SARS-CoV-2 reveals a dominant strain type with strong allergic associations : https://doi.org/10.1075/pnas.2007840117.*

**4.Jacob Kames, David D. Holcomb,Ofer Kimchi,Michael Dicuccio, Nobuko Hamasaki-Katagiri,Tonywang Anton A. Komar, Aikatorini Alexaki and Chava Kimchi Sarfaty : Seq*

**5. Huihui Wang ,Xuemei Li,Tao Li,,Shubing Zhang,Lianzi Wang, Xian Wu and Jiaging Liu : The genetic Sequence, origin and diagnosis of SARS-CoV-2 , Eur. J.Clin-Microbiol.Infect. Disease 2020 , Apr.24,1-7.*

**6. B. Coutard, C. Valle, Xide Lamballerie B. Cannord,N.G. Seidah and E. Decroly : The Spike glycoprotein of new Coronavirus 2019-nCoV contains a furin like cleavage site absent in CoV of the same Clade : ANTIVIRAL Res. 2020,176104742.*

**7.Vincent Racanello :Furin cleavage site in the SARS-CoV-2 Coronavirus glycoprotein : Virology@virology.ws/2020/13, Feb.2020.*

**8. Limeng Yan :SARS-CoV2-IS an unrestricted Bioweapon:A truth Revealed through uncovering a large*

***scale organized Fraud: Oct. 2020: https://www.researchgate.net/publication/344545028.***

****9.Javier A. James,Nicole M.Andire, Joshua S., Chappie,Jaan K. Millet and Gary R. Whittaker : Phylogenetic analysis and structural modeling * *10.Jian Huang and Lan Zhao : A high throughput –strategy for Covid-19 testing based o***n next generation sequencing : https://doi.org/ 10.1101/ 2020.06.12-20129718.

*11.Zarafshan Shiraz : Covid-19 Result of attempt to manufacture to AIDS Virus ? Nobel winning Scientist Sparks New Controversy.: 2020:India.com/Viral/Covid-19.

- ****Detection of a SARS-CoV-2 variant of concern in South Africa ;Nature volume 592, pages438–443 Published: 09 March 2021;Houriiyah Tegally, Eduan Wilkinson, Marta Giovanetti, Arash Iranzadeh, Vagner Fonseca, Jennifer Giandhari, DeelanDoolabh, Sureshnee Pillay,Emmanuel James San, Nokukhanya Msomi, Koleka Mlisana, Anne von Gottberg, Sibongile Walaza, MushalAllam, Arshad Ismail, Thabo Mohale, Allison J. Glass, Susan Engelbrecht, Gert Van Zyl, Wolfgang Preiser, FrancescoPetruccione,***

***Alex Sigal, Diana Hardie, Gert Marais, Tulio de Oliveira***

*Can Coronavirus Cause Heart Damage?*

***Infectious DiseasesReviewed By:Erin Donnelly Michos, M.D., M.H.S.*** Published on April 24, 2020***8. Limeng Yan :SARS-CoV2-IS an unrestricted Bioweapon:A truth Revealed through uncovering a large scale organized Fraud: Oct. 2020: https://www.researchgate.net/publication/344545028***

***9.Javier A. James,Nicole M.Andire, Joshua S., Chappie,Jaan K. Millet and Gary R. Whittaker : Phylogenetic analysis and structural modeling reveals an evolutionary distinct and Proteoloytically Sensitive activation Loop: J. Mol. Biol. 2021 , May 1,432(10),3309-3325.***

***10.Jian Huang and Lan Zhao : A high throughput –strategy for Covid-19 testing based on next generation sequencing : https://doi.org/ 10.1101/ 2020.06.12-20129718.***

***11.Zarafshan Shiraz : Covid-19 Result of attempt to manufacture to AIDS Virus ? Nobel winning Scientist Sparks New Controversy.: 2020:India.com/Viral/Covid-19.***

***1. 26, 2020.***

***2. Antonio Regalado(2018). Exclusive:Chinese Scientists are creating CRISPR babes :NATURE:BIOTECHNOLOGY:CRISPR.***

9 798890 027184

Printed by Libri Plureos GmbH in Hamburg,
Germany